Anti Rule

Navigating The Lies About Fiction Writing

Christian Francis

Echo On Publications

E-book: 978-1-916582-01-9
Paperback: 978-1-916582-05-7

Copyright © 2023 Christian Francis.
All Rights Reserved.

No part of this book may be reproduced in any form or by any electronic or mechanical means, including information storage and retrieval systems, without permission in writing from the publisher, except by a reviewer who may quote brief passages in a review.

ECHO ON
PUBLISHING

echohorror.com

Contents

Prologue	1
Foreword	3
CALLING MR LEONARD	11
THE JUNK RULES	19
Write what you know	20
Show, Don't Tell	22
Dialogue Tags	24
Balances	26
Head-Hopping	28
Active vs passive voice	31
Avoid Cliché	34
Avoid repetition	37
The Inciting Incident	39
THE WRITING PROCESS	41
When, where and how long to write	41
Research	43
Planning, Plotting and Pantsers	46
Three Act Structures	50
The Hero's Journey	51
Writer's block	53
Imposter Syndrome	55
Drafting	57
Transitional scenes	61
The Narrator	63
Where to start and end	65

Writing for Market	67
Writing for Market 2: Smaller Genre Marketability	70
SOME POSITIVITY...	75
About all the 'rules'	81
WHAT COMES NEXT...	85
Editing	85
What kind of publisher?	89
Literary agent or no literary agent	95
Queries and rejections	97
SELF-PUBLISHING POINTERS	101
eBooks - To flow or be fixed?	101
Book Covers	102
Licenses	104
Book Titles	105
Pull quotes	106
Blurbs	107
Going Wide	110
KDP vs Ingram vs Createspace vs Draft2Digital vs vs vs vs	111
Paper	115
ISBNs	115
Book Pricing	119
Marketing Mania	120
ARCs	124
Reviews	127
Influencers	130
Piracy	131
Community	134
Afterword	137

Prologue

It was a dark and stormy night. The clouds billowed with fury as they unleashed their almost biblical torrents upon the sleepy hamlet of Alcester that lay far below.

"I can't go out in that," Jacob mused loudly to himself as he stared out of the church's stained-glass window. Each word he spoke echoed throughout the hollowness of the building, reverberating against each of the centuries-old stone-clad walls. Walls that had witnessed many a passing storm, metaphorically and figuratively.

Then... A silence.

The rain stopped.

The thunder faded into the distance.

The wind quelled to nothing.

Christian Francis

A chill ran up Jacob's spine as a feeling of unease flooded his blood.

He barely had time to catch his breath when suddenly, and literally, all hell broke loose.

———

If you are confused about why there is a prologue, do not fret, you have not bought the wrong book. You will soon understand its purpose after you finish Chapter 1.

Foreword
Why I Wrote This Book

I know what you are thinking; why on earth should you read yet ANOTHER *how to write fiction* book? Well, this is unlike all those others you will have read. This is less of a 'guide' and more of a slap across your face.

This is a wake-up call with the intention of telling you that most of what you have been taught is wrong.

This book intends to illustrate how what has been taught by most writing teachers, authors, and editors is detrimental to the aspiring author's potential career. Plain and simple. I want to illustrate that what has been parroted by people in authority has forced the written art to become more tedious and homogenised. A tsunami of 'rules' and 'tips' now floods our existence. Little soundbites may *seem* at face value to be based in common sense and logic—especially if you are told this by a self-proclaimed 'expert'—but I am here to tell you that these teachings are, in the end, very damaging.

I seem overly dramatic by saying 'damaging', but I don't use that word lightly. I have spoken to many novice authors over the years who had quit their dreams before they had a chance to even start their stories, all *because* of what they were told regarding these 'rules' and 'tips'. It would not be an issue if it was just in one book or taught by one writing teacher, but these 'rules' and 'tips' are plastered on the pages of lauded writing guides and spoken by 'experts' all over social media. Each one of these arethe same. They all speak in a strict absolutist way and talk down on any notion that what they teach isn't the gospel truth and the only good way. A way that forces doubt into the creative method that all authors have, and if they feel they cannot follow these rules, they give up the dream. It's this kind of exclusionary behaviour I cannot stand.

You see, authors are an easy mark. We are, in general, a fragile bunch. We take reviews to heart. We take negativity personally. Why? Because what we produce is highly personal to us. It's a creation of our own making. And because we are like this, we are easy to make money from if you are a shyster salesman of the rhetoric that promises the world... *'Do you want to sell a million copies of your book? Here is how you do it! Do you want to know how to make your writing more marketable? Sign up for my course, and I'll teach you the secrets. Do you want to be a famous author? Let me tell you how! Now give me money.'* You've heard all this kind of stuff before. And it would be all well and good if they actually had any answers that could help you. But none ever do. They all regurgitate the exact words. The same 'rules' and 'tips'. But in the end, they don't know a thing. They just know how to take your money.

The genesis of all these teachings I am talking about came from long ago, made by those who wanted consistency in their product lines: Publishers. You see, writing used to be a closed profession, only accessible to a few. Self-publishing did not exist to the masses, so the landscape of authors was much smaller than it is today. So much so that it was considered that *only* the best could get an agent, *only* the best could get a publisher, and *only* the best could get a book deal. This was before the advent of the internet and the digital age, when book publishing was all print, and book publishing was a moneymaking goliath of an industry. Authors back then were even paid enough to live a *very* comfortable life. This kind of power meant that the publishers themselves were very, very influential. They controlled the written word. And each of these companies, like any company with a product line, demanded consistency Consistency is reliable.

Consistency means repeat business. Consistency means money.

This consistency ensured that all books they output were consistent in tone and voice. Soon all books began to *feel* the same to the reader. Not in terms of the actual story itself but in phrasing. The layout. The word usage. The structure. I get *why* they wanted all their books to read the same, as they wanted their customers to have a reliable experience and wanted their books to be understood and consumed by *every* person who had a wallet. A noble inclusive idea, sure, but in this, one crucial thing was lost: the author's unique voice.

Over time, editors, teachers, and authors adopted these rules as the *only* way for a person to write fiction. The *proper* way to write fiction. But none of them... *None* of those teaching these 'rules' and 'tips' were truly understanding what writing was. Instead, they taught writing as a business model instead of an actual art form.

Nowadays, a *lot* has changed. As self-publishing becomes accessible to all and the number of authors out there increases exponentially, no one is beholden to a publisher anymore; thus, no one should be beholden to their archaic rules for consistency.

Things, though, have taken a turn for the worse. People have not seen through the 'rules' and 'tips'. Instead, just more and more people are out there saying the same old stuff and teaching the same old tired lessons. Social media is packed full of people hawking the same words. Nothing changed with the market becoming bigger, nothing except more people wanting to know the truth and being fed the same lies.

We are in the age of the influencer, where an infinite number of people are preying on those desperate to learn the writing profession. These vultures look to make all the money they can from those wanting to become authors. Turn on any social media platform, from Twitter to TikTok, and you will see a barrage of posts, videos, and blogs that spew the same old teachings on writing fiction as if *they* invented them and are the only ones to have these breakthrough answers. Unlike before, none of this is being said to ensure consistency for some publisher's product line, but it is done for likes and in the hope of selling more of their own self-published *how-to* books. Books that are just rewordings of the billion other books out there, all covering the same topics. The ones that eschew these 'rules' and 'tips' are almost all verbatim to each other. These 'gurus' (as it seems they love calling themselves) teach with an air of self-assured confidence that people naturally believe. What's funnier about this is that these people claim to have the answers. They say that they have sold hundreds of thousands of books, so they are experts that you should listen to. But the only issue with this is that their best-selling books are *how-to* books. *How to* books about a topic they have no experience in. *How to* books that have zero original content. None contains any knowledge or genuine help for aspiring authors within their pages. All there is, is just the same old junk repeated ad nauseam. They are filled with pseudo-academic words, speaking in absolutes, spouting 'rules' and 'tips' like a machine gun at you. They are bombarding you with confusing yet convincing pointers.

It's not just those selling that are the problem; millions of people have propagated these same 'rules' and 'tips', not for want of money—but because they believe it. Editors. Authors. All saying the same stuff, speaking in absolutes and half-truths they don't even understand—mainly as they seem not to know any better. Even famous authors shout the same teachings as the only rules. The golden rules.

You have to remember that most people do not *understand* the craft. Sure, they may be able to write or edit. Sure, they may have even written or edited many best-selling books. But they need to *understand* the mechanics of writing as an art form. They only know how *they* write and edit. They confuse this with how art works and think what they do is all there is to it. And they do it all with the best possible intention.

Which brings us to this book. I am here to tell you that *nothing* they say can *really* help you. Sure, what they say sounds true. They are *very* confident. They may be *very* successful. And they all say the same things... So you should not blame yourself if you have believed them before or been disheartened by them...

A while back, I started making videos on TikTok, giving counterarguments to all these 'rules' and 'tips' to vent my frustration, and the reaction to them was incredible. I started to be contacted by hundreds of authors thanking me for dispelling what they had been taught. They told me that they had felt excluded from the craft and dissuaded from finishing their books, as they did not follow the golden rules out there, but after seeing my videos have found the passion again. It made me realise that many authors who have not seen my videos could be craving this kind of message, this assurance, from someone. As not everyone in the world is on TikTok, I decided to write this book so that any author out there who may feel browbeaten by 'rules' can see there is another way they could try, and should try.

It is why this isn't a massive tome of a book. This is a small and easily digestible pocket-book-sized guide to the basics. Something to give honest advice that will *help* an author on their journey. That is the hope I have for this, anyway.

At the end of the main part of the book, I have also included self-publishing tips, as there seems to be a wealth of misinformation out there, too, so I thought it would be best to include that kind of stuff to help people navigate the treacherous seas of what lies after writing.

I hope what I say within these few pages help. Keep in mind that I am not saying what rules you should follow. Any advice I give is my opinion because, when it all comes down to facts, your art is *your* art. I can only give pointers and show you what is wrong out there.

You may also realise that I call them authors, not writers. This is because there is a huge stigma to anyone new to the craft not feeling they can call themselves authors. You can. And I will call you that. You are an author if you want to be one. It's not a magic word reserved only for the few.

Calling Mr Leonard

The following is an excerpt from a 2001 *New York Times* article by Elmore Leonard, a lauded crime author. These were his ten rules for authors, as part of the paper's *Writers on Writing* series of articles.

1. *Never open a book with weather.*
2. *Avoid prologues.*
3. *Never use a verb other than "said" to carry dialogue.*
4. *Never use an adverb to modify the verb "said,"...he admonished gravely.*
5. *Keep your exclamation points under control. You are allowed no more than two or three per 100,000 words of prose.*
6. *Never use the words "suddenly" or "all hell broke loose."*
7. *Use regional dialect, patois, sparingly.*
8. *Avoid detailed descriptions of characters.*

9. *Don't go into great detail describing places and things.*
10. *Try to leave out the part that readers tend to skip.*

These rules each look normal at first glance. I mean, he was a very famous author, right? He has a legion of fans. He *would* know these things, you would think. His advice is solid and should be listened to, right? *Right?*

Wrong.

Very wrong.

So very wrong.

Sure, he could write a book. He wrote many. He was a very successful author. But these 'rules' prove he had zero understanding of the craft. His advice was solely a bunch of arbitrary ideas and ill-thought-out musings he got paid to put together. Then, because of who he was, people took what he wrote onboard as the only way to write, and it must be the true path to any writing success.

I will break his rules down to better illustrate how terrible they really are.

Never open a book with weather.

Why? What possible reason is there to follow this? Because somehow he thought that was a cliché

Anti Rule

thing to do. Well, cliché is *not* a bad thing. It's comfortable. And as a start of a book, a cliché can be a needed start to a story's journey. Also, the weather can be a foreshadowing. It can set a scene perfectly. It can juxtapose the scene that follows. It's a writing *tool*. Saying *never do it* is a stupid thing to declare and a stupid thing to believe.

Avoid prologues.

Some stories need prologues. *Game of Thrones, A Tale of Two Cities, Jurassic Park, The Hitchhikers Guide to the Galaxy*. All books with spectacular prologues, which are a needed part of the book. This advice to avoid them is ridiculous, and you should definitely have a prologue if your story benefits from one. No story is the same.

Never use a verb other than "said" to carry dialogue.

This is the most stupid advice. I will discuss this more in the section about dialogue tags later on; suffice to say, if a reader uses 'said' for every tag, their writing would be more boring.

Never use an adverb to modify the verb "said,"…he admonished gravely.

Again… A stupid, stupid rule. Modifying a dialogue tag can make the writing better. Look at the example he used. *He admonished gravely*. He thought that proved his point when it, in fact, proved him wrong. It is actually a well-written dialogue tag and tells you more than just *he said*.

Keep your exclamation points under control. You are allowed no more than two or three per 100,000 words of prose.

Here's a tip... if someone is teaching you about writing and says the words *you are not allowed,* you can ignore everything else they say. You are allowed to write whatever the hell you want!!!!

Never use the words "suddenly" or "all hell broke loose."

Oh my... Again, you can see how this is a bunch of B.S., right? Never use the word *suddenly*? Wow...

Use regional dialect, patois, sparingly.

Way to show your arrogance, Mr. Leonard. Way to reduce a different culture to nothing. *If* you have a regional dialect or different culture in your book, it *has* to be authentic. You *do not* have to water your writing down because of this insulting and frankly xenophobic 'rule'. Just because he preferred that all his writing was without any reality and was easy to read does not mean anyone should kowtow to his words. Books should engage. They should not be easy. What I mean by that can be illustrated by the book *Feersum Endjin* by Iain Banks. In it, Banks had a character that wrote his parts of the book in phonetics as that character was dyslexic and could not write in any other way. This is a remarkable achievement in writing. Sure, it is challenging to read, but that is its genius. That is an author's creative voice using a writing style to build the story. Okay, it is not a regional dialect, but it follows the same principle. And proves that this rule is junk.

Avoid detailed descriptions of characters. Don't go into great detail describing places and things.

I put these two rules as one... Can you see how stupid they are?

Tolkien? Woolf? King? Hemingway? They were obviously all wrong, and their books should be rewritten. Mr. Leonard has spoken! You must all read what I am about to write and remember it... detail as much as you want for the scenes you are writing to be fully realised! *You* are the storyteller. *You* are the narrator. This is *your* voice.

Try to leave out the part that readers tend to skip.

Mr. Leonard... Now, I know that you are dead, but if you had books where people seemed to skip certain parts, then I think those parts were poorly written and boring.

Christian Francis

Don't tarnish anyone else with your inadequacies.

Elmore Leonard may have been a nice man. I have no idea. I don't rate his books; I find them all quite dull. But all I say above is about him as a teacher telling others how to write. His advice proved he had no idea of what he was doing. He had no idea of how to give actual advice. Personal opinion is *not* advice. What he thought, though mostly misguided and far off point, was valid to *him*. And you can believe what you want. But, when you publish these thoughts as a *how to write* , you are taking on a responsibility to the novice authors out there. You must ensure that your words are true and honest about the craft. What Mr. Leonard did was not true and he had nothing real to say about how to write or the variety of people out there wishing to learn.

You may be reading this thinking, *Oh, but that's just one guy*. But that's the issue; he is not just one guy. This is just one small example of the broader issues. You see, as soon as one person says it, and they carry any authority with them, then people assume that it's all true. Then those words spread. Then, they are adopted by anyone looking for things to sell or teach. Not because they are true words but because it's good content.

Don't believe me? Just look at the number of websites that have republished Mr.

Leonards's rules on writing as fact. Not one critical essay about how it's all baloney.

I hope you can now appreciate the prologue for this book; it was written just for Mr. Leonard.

The Junk Rules

Here is a way to know what to avoid when it comes to any writing advice given to you; Anyone who couches their writing rules with '*never*' or some other absolute is wrong. If they say that if you apply what they teach, your writing will be better, and ignoring these rules makes what you write amateur, you need to immediately discount everything that person will ever say.

You see, every story is different. Every author is different. Every genre is different. Every author's culture and experiences are different. There are no absolutes. There are no rules that apply to all. What works for one book will not work for another.

If anyone speaks any rules in absolutes, then they do not know what they are saying. I don't care who you are; I don't care how many books you have sold. Ignore any advice that uses an absolute.

There. Are. No. Absolutes.

Christian Francis

Write what you know

Possibly the worst advice anyone can give a fiction author.

Unless your story is based on events that happened to you, do not, I repeat, do not write what you know. Write what you can *imagine*.

Unless you are writing for market, you should write a story that surprises you as an author. You should write a story that delights you. If you are writing an erotic book, you should write what turns you on and what *could* turn you on. If you are writing a horror, don't just write about monsters you are familiar with; write about monsters that don't yet exist.

Writing is *creation*.

Writing is *living dreams as words*.

Write a story that makes you nervous.

Write a story that makes you laugh out loud.

Let your mind and imagination tell a story you had no idea you could come up with.

Anything less is dulling the enjoyment that can come with the craft.

Here is the best advice I ever got about writing: "If you write something that shocks and surprises you, the reader will feel that same tenfold." That was not actually said to me but instead written in pencil on the inside of an old how-to-write guide I had back in college. I have no idea who wrote it or why, but I have found that to be truer than anything printed on the pages of the book it was written in. Basically, tell the story that *you* want to read, not one that you *think* you should tell.

Whether you are a plotter or a pantser, your story should make you feel something. It should be a story that you crave to know the ending of. It should be a story that you can't wait to write.

Why should you not write what you know? The sad truth is that you know *very little*. Every person knows little. Even the most genius people know very little in the grand scheme of existence. Most people know nothing of other sexes. They know nothing of other people's jobs. They know nothing of how things actually work.

Write what you know? Pah! That's not only a totally impractical writing rule. It's boring.

Can you imagine what a story would be like to read if it was just about that tiny bit of experience of your life? I will reiterate if your book is literally about your experiences, then that is different. I am talking about fiction. (I felt I had to say that again to be clear)

Write what you *need* to know.

Let your amazing brain work on creating something beautiful.

Research the facts you need to find out. The rest... is creation.

Show, Don't Tell

One of the most ludicrous of the 'golden rules' and one that most teachers, editors, and authors seem oblivious to the stupidity of.

The ones that preach this rule will say that the playwright Anton Chekov originated *Show Don't Tell* when he wrote, *'Don't tell me the moon is shining; show me the glint of light on broken glass!'*

He never said this.

He actually said, *'In descriptions of nature, one must seize on small details, grouping them so that when the reader closes his eyes, he gets a picture. For instance, you'll have a moonlit night if you write that on the mill dam, a piece of glass from a broken bottle glittered like a bright little star, and that the black shadow of a dog or a wolf rolled past like a ball.'*

He wanted authors to bask in the descriptions of the majesty of nature. To delve into the beauty of it as much as possible using a narrator's voice to describe the hidden wonders in a typical scene beyond the standard description. Doing the

Anti Rule

opposite of what the *Show Don't Tell* rules tell you to do.

My main issue with *Show Don't Tell* is that it was, and should stay, aimed at plays and films. It is a rule for visual media, not fiction books. But it has still erroneously become a mainstay of writing rules. Saying that you need to do less narration and rely on your character's actions and dialogue to tell the story.

No.

Never.

NO, NO, NO!

To all authors out there, ignore this rule in its entirety. It holds no value to writing. Of course, a scene you write may be better with less narrative information or to change to dialogue, but a blanket rule does not apply to *your* story. Some stories need the *tell* part to be at the forefront always. Fantasy and Sci-Fi books revel in *tell,* and all the better for them. But they also will need *show*.

It all depends on the scene, genre, narrator's voice, the characters, the plot etc.

Can you imagine how boring a book would be if the story were not led by a narrator saying what was happening?! It would be detached and cold and, quite frankly, boring. And that's what you would end up with because all those teaching this teach it as an absolute that you have to *show, show, show*! When you don't. The real education should be that you need to show *or* tell *depending on your story or scene*. Using *show* a lot would inevitably miss out on needed information that character actions could not possibly detail. It would essentially withhold information from the reader and make the scene almost a summation without any poetry or feeling. All because of this pointless 'rule'.

I've heard people say, *'Oh, but using too much tell slows down the scene!'* And? So? How is that a bad thing? This is not an action film where you must fit in a bazillion stunts into one minute of footage. It's a book where the author is telling the story at *their* pace, not at a pace a rule in your mind has arbitrarily set.

Dialogue Tags

I should probably just write all these down in a list and say ignore all of the above, but I feel I have to say why, to try and show you how silly it is that so many people spout these 'rules'.

Rules about dialogue tags are my pet hate, and they really, *really* annoy me. It is yet another 'golden rule' that strips the author's voice away from the sentence.

Anti Rule

They say that you should only use 'said', 'asked' or 'replied' as a tag to dialogue, as they are invisible to the reader and will improve the writing flow .

What utter balls.

I have dealt with editors, beta readers, authors, and publishers who have all at one time told me that I should follow this advice. They say *they* know. That my story would benefit from it. And every time I tell them 'no thank you' (in a more expletive way, of course). This rule does *not* make the writing more professional, less amateur, or more commercial.

Ok, I will stop being polite now... F**k off to all and sundry who believe all authors must follow this rule. I would much rather write and read a story with emotive dialogue tags. I don't want words to be invisible. I want to *feel* a story. Not gloss over words to rush to the next sentence, like it's all some kind of race. These people claim it's professional, but they also believe you should never use non-verbal words as a dialogue tag.

"Go eat a bag of dicks," Christian sneered.

Now I will write that as *they* say I should—all to be more professionally written.

"Go eat a bag of dick," Christian said, sneering.

They talk about avoiding useless words, and adding *said* does nothing except be less emotive and add an extra word in for no reason. Non-verbal tags *work*. They can add to the feeling of the dialogue. They can make the reader see more. Know more.

"This rule is so boring," Christian yawned.

Vs.

"This rule is so boring," Christian said, yawning.

The non-verbal tag is more compelling, reads better, and is immediate.

Basically, dialogue tags can be whatever is best to tell that scene or describe that moment. Never let anyone tell you that otherwise is amateur. As it is not. It is just yet another arbitrary rule that people have made up. If it were not, their reasoning would make some logical sense, but it does not. At all. Not even a little bit.

Balances

Why do some people think dialogue and narrative description have a singular balance? This is not an old rule I am debunking, but one that a lot of new editors and writing tutors (mainly based on the internet) are guilty of. Again, because they do not understand the craft and are making videos or posting things for likes and to expand their content.

The old rule was actually a pretty helpful one; If your scene needs to move fast; use less description, use much shorter sentences and rely on more concise dialogue from your characters. Simple, yet very effective.

But the advice I have seen out there again and again is that your book needs to be about 50% dialogue and 50% description—all to keep your reader engaged, apparently.

You can immediately forget this, as they do not even understand what a story is made of.

A scene may need much dialogue.

A scene may need little dialogue.

A scene may need no dialogue.

It depends on the scene.

It depends on the story.

It depends on the author.

It depends on the genre.

If someone reads your book, be they a paid professional or a friend, and they feel that one section of your book may be too dialogue heavy or too light, listen to their concerns about why. If you agree, you can change it. If you do not, then just thank them for their feedback.

There is no balance in writing dialogue and description that can evenly apply to all books. It can only apply to one scene within one chapter of one book. Remember that. Your book is a journey. It will have fast bits. It will have slow bits. It will have peaks and troughs of pacing.

So, if you don't listen to their balance rule, how can you know how fast a moment in a book should be? The simple answer is that you will know when you hear your story told back to you. That is the best way to check the pace. Getting others' feedback is invaluable, but it is only their opinion, and they are not the author. An author who may be unsure, upon hearing their story read back to them, will be able to see any issues clearly. How? Because they will have seen countless tv shows and films and read a wealth of books. They will know a comfortable story pace instinctively, even if they don't realise that they do. New authors know a lot more than they give themselves credit for. In this day and age, storytelling is everywhere, and we were all raised on it. With distance from your book and reading it with fresh eyes, any imbalance that is needed would be easily seen.

(For getting your story read back to you, you can use text-to-voice sites, or record it yourself and play it back. More on this later.)

Head-Hopping

What is head-hopping? It is the change of a character's viewpoint (or point of view/POV)

Anti Rule

within the middle of a scene within a chapter. The rule is that you should only have one viewpoint within a single scene.

My issue is that many people teaching this rule do not fully understand what they are saying. This is evident when they make no differentiation between head-hopping and omniscient narration at the outset. Omniscient narration can jump into character thoughts at will, detailing multiple POVs in the third person. This is not only ok but commonplace as a narration tool. Any new author listening to this 'rule' could easily be convinced that omniscient narration *is* head-hopping, which it most definitely is not.

The thought that one scene should only have one viewpoint is restrictive for zero reasons. The concern is that it would confuse the reader if first person POV switches in a scene. Why? Keep in mind that the same people laying out this 'rule' are the same ones who say that your reader is intelligent and should not be talked down to. Well, what is it? Are they intelligent or so stupid that they cannot understand a switching

POV?

The real and only part of this that is actually helpful is a very quick and simple thing to remember; if you switch POV within a scene, preface the switch by notifying the reader that the character has changed. Simple.

Here is head-hopping done in a confusing way to read:

Is that all there is to it? James mused silently, as Ingrid walked up behind him, thinking almost the same thing. *That's almost too simple?*

Do you see that you cannot properly see who thought the second part? So instead, you would write:

Is that all there is to it? James mused silently.

Ingrid walked up behind him, also thinking to herself, *That's almost too simple?*

Her silent words echoed his unknowingly.

Basically, treat the changing POV as you would dialogue. Make sure the tags are clear. That's it.

Anyone who says you cannot head-hop in a scene should tell that to Jane Austen or JRR Tolkien. You just need to make it clear what is happening.

The head-hopping rule is a rule for the sake of a rule. Virtually all rules for dialogue are more or less the same rules for character POV thoughts. (Aside from not having speech marks on them and putting them in italics.)

Why even have this rule if many beloved and famous authors don't pay any attention to it? Because it is yet another way to enforce uniformity that should never have been implemented in the first place.

Active vs passive voice

Active voice; when the sentence's subject performs an action on the action's target in that order. *Jack picked up the bucket.*

Passive voice; the target of the action is the main focus, and the verb acts upon the subject. *The bucket was picked up by Jack.*

Before I start this, I have to state that I *adore* Stephen King. I honestly believe he is one of the best storytellers to have ever existed on this planet. I also recommend his book *'On Writing: A Memoir of the Craft'*. I find it an excellent insight into his process. But at the same time, I find some of his 'advice' quite misguided and insulting.

This is a man who will tell you that your writing needs to be quick and get to the point... But he is also an author who will never follow that advice. His books may be excellent, but they are *never* quick or to the point.

For this section, I have brought King up as he lays down a pretty steadfast rule regarding active and passive voice: *'You should avoid the passive voice... I think timid writers like them for the same reason timid lovers like passive partners. The passive voice is safe.'*

His view here is misguided as he gives an absolute to all authors and tries to insult them into following his way. Somehow insinuating that an active voice is braver and riskier and saying a passive voice is safe and boring.

No doubt you will, during your writing career, use a spelling and grammar checker like *Grammarly* or *Pro Writing Aid*. They will likely throw up a passive voice error when checking your writing, telling you that active voice is better. Insinuating like spelling, there's only one way to do it.

The reality is that this is all nonsense. A mix of active and passive voice is fine and can shift from scene to scene, depending on many factors.

Stephen King also gives an example in his book that he believes proves his point:

"*My first kiss will always be recalled by me as how my romance with Shayna was begun.* A simpler way to express this idea—sweeter and more forceful as well—might be this: *My romance with Shayna began with our first kiss. I'll never forget it.*"

My issue is that, while his active voice example is shorter and to the point, it is also colder. It is more basic. It is without any charm or author's voice. It limits the sentence to short and sharp bursts. Whereas his first example proves that the passive voice has many benefits in writing. You see, most passive voice sentences are generally longer and less direct than in active voice. They are more poetic and lyrical and can come across to the reader as warm and more involving.

If you want your scene to progress at a quicker pace, an active voice is one way to go. No doubt. But an active voice within a scene where the pace has to be gentle, subtle, and more deliberate in its pace could ruin it.

Fantasy, epic, and romance novels rely on passive voice to provide a kind of dreamlike air to the narration. The description in a passive voice allows the reader to be swept up and lost within the author's language.

The use of passive voice has *nothing* to do with being a timid author, just as active has nothing to do with being a bold author.

It's not just King. In the famous writing book "*The Elements of Style*" by William Strunk & E. B. White. The authors say the '*active voice is usually more direct and vigorous.*' They say that authors should only use active and never passive voice. Just like King, Strunk and White are wrong. (Their book, for the record, is also a tome of similar writing lies. So please avoid it, no matter what anyone tells you.)

You may think, *but Stephen King is famous, and The Elements of Style is a best seller; why should I not listen to them?* Well, just because you are famous does not mean you are right. Charles Dickens, William Shakespeare, Jane Austen. All three used passive voice to great acclaim. And each is a lot more famous than King, Strunk or White. But this is *not* the fame game. (I will reiterate that I am a huge King fan) This is about the English language and its uses and the advice they have given. The absolute rules they say about this subject are just wrong and poorly considered.

With all that in mind, I implore this; Use passive voice. Use active voice. Use both. Not either. Just ensure that you use each to their best advantage. An active voice for a more fast and immediate moment. A passive voice for a slower and more involving scene. That is all you should consider.

Avoid Cliché

Many rules I may disagree with, yet I understand. I may get where they came from; I just don't think they are good or meaningful to an author, especially a novice. This one, however… I have no idea why people ever demanded that this was a rule you must follow. It just does not make any sense. Even the dictionary badly describes what a cliché is:

Cliché - a phrase or opinion that is overused and betrays a lack of original thought.

Whoa there! That's some harsh talk there, Mr. Dictionary.

Cliché is *not* bad.

There I said it. Why? Because in writing, a cliché is almost always also a trope, unless it's a phrase.

Trope - a significant or recurrent theme; a motif.

Before you start getting on your high horse saying that a trope and a cliché are different, hear me out.... Here are some things that are famously labelled as plot clichés:

- ***The love triangle*** - Most romance stories use this.
- ***The chosen one -*** Most sci-fi and fantasy use this.
- ***Parents who are abusive or absentee*** - I just don't get this one... So? It's a fact of life. How is that a cliché? Is someone driving a car in a movie cliché to you too?
- ***A first-person narrator describing themselves in the mirror*** - Uh... What? This is just stupid.

Most of these are tropes. Not clichés. To make matters worse, here is what they say your writing is, should you use a cliché; Lazy.

What a nerve! How dare they! They have zero idea

about the craft. Your book is not a sum of any clichés or tropes you have used. Your story *may* contain them but should not be defined by them. The fact that anyone says not to use something so arbitrary proves they do not understand writing. Period. They boil everything down to the most basic forms without looking at the wider picture of storytelling. The harsh truth is that there is nothing new to write, yet they teach that your book needs to be a story never dreamt of before. When in fact, all stories are based on others, even if not consciously.

There is no originality left, just fresh spins, and it's those spins where the new excitement lies.

Clichés are part of the human experience. Love and horror stories are, by and large, based on cliché. Clichés are comforting. They are familiar. They have to be used in places to allow the reader to easily fall into the narrative and be swept along.

Sure, clichés in set-up may be predictable, but the story you tell, unbridled of rules, will end up somewhere new. Somewhere original.

So, use your cliches and tropes with pride. You may have a *chosen one* narrative, but it's not the fact you use this trope/cliché; it's what you do with it. It's that fresh spin you put on it. The way you frame it. The way you tell it. The author's voice holds all the originality.

Now let's look at cliché phrases:

- *The wrong side of the bed.*
- *Think outside the box.*
- *Loose cannon.*
- *A chip off the old block.*
- *A clean slate.*
- *A perfect storm.*
- *Can of worms.*
- *What goes around comes around.*
- *Dead as a doornail.*
- *Plenty of fish in the sea.*

I will say this once as clearly as I can. Your character can talk however they want. If your character says a cliché? So what? Humans do that. It's not only typical but expected of conversive language. Saying never to use cliché phrases is nonsensical. It is in our language. It is commonplace. It can be used if the author wishes their character to say it.

Avoid repetition

Really? Really? That's your advice? Really?

Christian Francis

As you can guess, repetition has a place in writing, just as cliché. Repetition bolsters and reinforces views and story ideas. Don't avoid it if your writing needs it.

One of my fondest memories of dealing with a terrible editor was when they gave me some terrible advice. Advice that immediately made me stop working with them.

The phrase in question that caused the issue was:

"I knew you were going to do that." Jenna's words dripped with an evil glee as a lascivious smile crept over her wasting face.

The editor wrote on the manuscript in a red Sharpie:

NO, NO, NO, NO. It should be

"I knew you were going to do that," Jenna said with a lascivious smile.

We know the woman is old. This needless repetition is amateur.

It wasn't the rudeness. It wasn't them acting superior with their tone. It was their point about repetition. It made me stop working with them immediately. So what if I had mentioned something in my writing before? I wanted to repeat it. Why? Repetition reinforces. It can embolden description. Repetition works. Repetition works. Repetition works. Get it? As to why I was so quick to stop working with this editor? It is easy to see if someone doesn't get your writing, and there would be no benefit to either me or the editor to carry on.

The *only* time repetition should be avoided is when you are repeating something you should not. Like a character mistakenly repeating an action when they just did that action. Or a scene repeating because of a cut-and-paste error. That's all. The rest is the author's voice. You may look back on your writing and think that a description is being told again and wish to cut that. That is your choice to do. But never cut it just because of this rule. If you feel that the repetition is needed, then keep it.

The Inciting Incident

They say you should have an inciting incident in the first 25% of your book. They say that you should set the scene, then introduce characters, and then have the inciting incident happen as soon as you can.

I, of course, do not agree.

I have some advice, but ultimately it's your story to tell how you want.

My opinion is, why even have the inciting incident in the book at all? It's rarely that interesting to read and is better served if it happens just *before* the start of the book. Open your story when it has just happened. After the virus has been released. After the meteor hit. After the wife leaves the husband. After the death of whoever. Scene-setting and character-building can be done as the story progresses,—after the inciting incident. This way, the reader is immediately in the story. Hooked from the start. Besides, the most exciting part of the story is what happens after the incident anyway!

But no, having a book told in a rigid scene set—character, build—inciting incident way is dull. Tell it a different way! Be original.

———

In all, you can see a common thread. All these 'Rules' and 'tips' you have heard are nothing more than the arbitrary opinion of a few people who do not understand the wonderous variety of the writing craft. They are taught to make your book the same as someone else's. This is not good advice to anyone new starting the writing journey.

The 'rules' and 'tips' don't stop there, oh no. They also cover the physical *how-to* process of writing...

The Writing Process

Not content with teaching arbitrary, incomplete, and non-sensical things to write writing tutors and all people like that also try to tell you how to write...

When, where and how long to write

This is a strange subject to even discuss. It's insane to me to think that any advice needs to be discussed about this subject. I have seen a lot of advice from so-called professionals out there. Conflicting advice.

You must write as soon as you wake up!

You must write in the evenings only!

You must write solidly for X number of hours a day!

Keep writing. Don't stop. Treat writing like a job.

Write only in a dedicated writing space.

No.

No.

No.

No.

Hell no.

Again more advice that is tone-deaf to reality. Writing is a craft. It's an art. And every artist is different. Some people can write for 10 hours straight. Some can only write for 10 minutes a day. Some people write in the early morning. Some at night. Some write on the toilet. Some write on their phone whilst waiting to pick their kids up from soccer practice. No one is the same, and no one is wrong.

I'll say it again... There is no right way or wrong way. Writing is an art, and artists can create art however they want.

There is some advice, though, that you should follow regarding how an author should physically prepare to write; *"Do back exercises. Pain is distracting."* The brilliant

Margaret Atwood said this, and it's probably the best advice. As an author who has hunched over a keyboard for years and now has a bad back, I can attest to this being a golden rule all should not gloss over but should start as soon as possible. Aside from that, when it comes to where, when, and how long you should write? There is no correct answer. It is whatever works best for you. You may only be able to write for an hour a year, and if so, fine. It doesn't make you less of an author, however long you write for.

Research

Many authors I have spoken to seem to think there is only one reason to research for a fiction book: For the reader's sake. I've heard the argument that when it comes down to it, research is not for the author's benefit. An author can write whatever they want, right? They can say that there are snowstorms in Malta every June if they choose. It actually doesn't matter if anything is factual in fiction, does it?

Well, I guess, in theory, it shouldn't. But in practice, it does. I agree with the writing tutors on this one.

Authors *should* research. 100% they should. Here are two reasons why... The first is the standard reason that is taught to writers:

They should ensure that real places, events, and people used in their stories are true to life. Why? Because most fiction stories exist in the real world, and you want that reality to be as accurate and factual as possible so that the reader can connect with your story and anything incorrect isn't jarring to the story being told. If you read even a fiction book and a real-world fact is demonstrably false, it drags the reader out of the story. If you have a medical procedure in your novel, you better be sure it's true to life and use the correct terminology, or there will be a revolt on your hands from readers!

Here is what I see as the main reason:

Research is not just for the factual but also the invented. Many fantasy and sci-fi authors use real word history as a basis for their worlds, and many authors research for inspiration into characters, plot points, you name it. Research is a key to inspiration.

Never underestimate how much picking up a non-fiction book can help you with ideas! For me, the kinds of books I could not do without are about old beliefs and mythology. Forgotten stories of old-world monsters have fed into my writing so much.

And no matter how much you *think* you know of a subject, trust me, you know little, and there is much more to discover. Personally, I know a lot about mythological horror. Horror is my genre. But I always find out new fascinating facts that set my brain on fire with inspiration when I do more research. (As an aside, the book *"The Encyclopaedia of Things That Never Were"* by Michael Page and Robert Ingpen is one of the best books for horror and fantasy inspiration)

But you do not *have* to research when it could impede your creativity... I am, of course, talking of when research becomes less about the creation and more about the market. When I wrote my YA horror *'The Dead Woods'*, I was told beforehand that I must research the market. I must see what other YA horror authors are doing to ensure I ride the right trend. I took exception to this.

Why would I need to research for this? Just because it's a younger audience? Do they think I can't write a book without cynically checking others' work for ways to sell things in this market?

You may think at first hand that I am being a bit silly by refusing to research, but look at it this way;

- I have written many horror novels, so I know how to write horror.
- I am writing for a younger audience; therefore, I know that the main characters should be young, so the intended reader can better identify.
- I know that sex is not appropriate subject to include in a book for a young audience.
- I know that excessive violence is a no-no.
- I know that harsh swearing is a no-no, too.

So what exactly am I supposed to research? This is my fiction. Fiction is the key word. It is a story. My story. And I know the general rules for a younger audience, as it's the same when you speak to anyone that age. Do you really need to research trends? That is called writing for market.

So when you *think* you must research anything, check your brain first. Is the research for the sake of fact-checking? Then research. Is it for the sake of marketability?

Then do as you prefer; just use your intelligence.

More on writing for market a little bit later...

Planning, Plotting and Pantsers

Nearly all writing teachers say the same thing. They say you need to work out your story beforehand. They say you need to intricately plan each and every aspect of your book, chapter by chapter. They say you need to work out the beginning, middle and end. They say you need to ensure that you know each and every character and that your character's arcs conform within a set three-act structure.

There are other ways.

I am *not* saying that anyone planning everything is wrong. Some authors have to plan things out entirely before they put pen to paper or finger to keyboard. It's how they process it all and keep track. But this method of plotting is enforced on all aspiring authors. Even authors who are not natural

Anti Rule

plotters are told they have to write in one way—the only true way for the book to be any good. But for people whose brain does not connect with this level of plotting, it can have a detrimental effect on their final story, as they end up telegraphing all of the plot far too much. Any surprise developments become too easily presumed beforehand by the reader, and most of all, the experience becomes a chore and not a passion.

Plotting is recommended when writing a story within a classroom setting so the teacher can work on storytelling mechanics. For writing something as part of a collective, like in a writing room for a TV show or film. Plotting is recommended. For a complicated book that is part of a bigger series, where an author feels they need to keep track of all the interconnecting strands. Plotting is recommended. For the rest, it is only one method.

You may have guessed I am what is called a pantser A pantser writes without plotting or planning and experiences the story as they write. That doesn't mean there is zero idea of what I am writing. I have a plan. It's just vague and changeable if the plot suddenly demands it. I am two steps ahead of my story; I just don't map it all out, nor know where it will end. I may have a rough idea, but it almost always concludes differently than I envisioned.

I encourage all authors to at least try this way once. You can still map everything out; just be amenable to change if you write a scene that begins to deviate from the set guide. Follow that thread. It could take you somewhere extraordinary. Sure, it can be scary for an author who feels that planning is the only way to write, but deviations can be rewarding. You may surprise yourself with where your story leads you. And if you ensure that each chapter section you write has something *you* find to be cool within it, maybe a plot turn that excites you, then the reader will feel as excited to read it. It can make your story fresher and less telegraphed.

For me, any intricate planning can stop my stories from developing in unforeseen and more original ways. At a planning stage, if I have all my characters and scenes mapped out, I feel I have done so without really knowing my characters or experiencing who they have become on the page— as no amount of preparation will show me who these characters truly are until they have been written. Planning is colder for me. More methodical. Writing, as I do, is emotional and becomes part of what I am creating. And as that happens, my characters develop in different ways, organically changing the arcs that I may have worked out for them. This is just me, however. This is my method.

For those people just learning and don't know what to do regarding planning. Do what feels comfortable to *you*. You may want to plan it all out, start writing, and then not use that plan as a rigid rule, but only as a starting point. You may want to plan and stick to it. You may wish to freestyle pantser-style... You may want to do a mix of all this... It is something that you need to figure out for yourself, but ensure one thing... make sure you try *every* way. Always remember, no matter what, *write with passion*. No matter the genre. No matter the story. Get excited by writing each chapter and each character. If you have no excitement, the writing will be blander for it. And if you can only write by planning every step beforehand, that's great. Just know... it's not the only way!

Social media has been flooded with authors—mainly plotters—proudly stating that pantsers are wrong and plotting is the only way. Do not be one of those people. You can create art any way you want. There is no right method.

For a better view... Here are some famous pantsers: George R R Martin, Stephen

King, Isaac Asimov, Margaret Atwood, Neil Gaiman, Mark Twain, Clive Barker, Diana Gabaldon, Dean Koonz... Now you people who believe plotting is the only and best way... Are you going to tell these authors that?

Three Act Structures

This one infuriates me. Writing teachers and editors have taken on the three-act structure as gospel for fiction. That all books must follow the rule.

The three-act structure is a model used in storytelling that divides a story into three parts/acts. These are *the Setup, the Confrontation*, and *the Resolution*. It is popularly considered that this came from Aristotle, who mused that every tragedy needs a beginning, middle and end. But he was not talking about writing, just about life. He was a philosopher, after all.

The act structure was originally formed for plays, which generally had two acts, but with the advent of film, the acts became part of the storytelling arc, and did not need intermissions to separate them.

In 1979 Syd Field wrote *Screenplay: The Foundations of Screenwriting*, where he brought the three-act structure idea into the mainstream. He talked about how all writing needs to follow the structure to be effective. But he was talking about screenplay writing.

Not fiction. Not novels.

It seems that many writing teachers still say that all books *must* follow the three acts. They are (as nicely as I can put it) so f**king wrong.

A book has no time limit. A book has no budget. A book does not have to tell the story as succinctly as possible. A book can tell multiple stories at once. Multiple stories within a book can each have their own beginning, middle, and end. Also, a book may not need a beginning. The story could start in the middle. It could start at the end.

The main issue with the three-act structure is that you can retroactively force the structure onto any book written. And boy, how writing teachers adore doing this. They will break down a popular book as a graph and say, *look, it's a three-act structure, so you must do that too*. You must remember, though, that they do not understand what they are saying. Placing a three-act structure onto a novel does not mean the author wrote it as such. What they have done is force their academic analysis onto something. Why is this misleading? Because every book has a beginning, a middle, and an end. Every book has a three-act structure if you break them apart enough.

Not content with telling you all this, they also say that each act must have the hero's journey...

The Hero's Journey

I am tired of analysis being mistaken for rules about how to write. Just because a story can be broken apart and the main characters' journey mapped out and forced into a journey path template means nothing to the author or the writing process. It's analysis only.

The hero's journey was popularised in 1949 by Joseph Campbell in his book *The Hero with a Thousand Faces*. He based his ideas on mythological storytelling research as well as philosopher and religious teaching. He wrote most famously about heroic archetypes in mythology.

"A hero ventures forth from the world of common day into a region of supernatural wonder: fabulous forces are there encountered, and a decisive victory is won: the hero comes back from this mysterious adventure with the power to bestow boons on his fellow man."

This is a fine summation in general terms. But only general terms.

He went into great detail with the seventeen stages of the journey, starting with the *Call To Adventure and* then going through many other story stages that are all quite vague and can be transplanted onto most character arcs.

This whole idea is all blown apart by the fact that Campbell was not an expert in his field and has been criticised by actual mythology experts who denounce his ideas as basic and flawed. They say he did not understand the mythology he was researching. But no one listened to the critics; they just loved Campbell's book. His idea of the hero's journey was taught as the only way to write a book.

Want to know the flaws with the hero's journey?

- It only looks at a masculine journey.
- It is only the journey of someone who has social advantages and privileges
- It is a very old-school way of looking at a character.

Like the three-act structure, the hero's journey is an analytical theory that was never intended to guide how to write fiction, and anyone who teaches this as the way to write is misrepresenting the source material without any critical eye.

Writer's block

You *will* get writer's block. You *will* hit a brick wall in a story. You will also invariably look up ways to get over it. The problem is that no one can cure it for you. No matter what they say. It is yet another thing that people claim to be able to address.

Here are some of the tips you may read about writer's block:

Write through it - That's like telling someone with no legs to walk it off.

Christian Francis

Writer's block doesn't exist - Only people who are not authors would say that, or someone just trying to be controversial for likes.

Take a break - Writer's block in a story is not just because of time and space. It is not there just because of the moment. A break will not do a lot; you need to do more than that.

Jump ahead of the story and write something that comes later, not caring if it fits - If the person who thought this ever met an author, they would know that doing this is not possible for many authors, as writer's block comes with anxiety about the whole book. It's not just this one scene anymore; when writer's block hits, it causes most authors to doubt everything they do and everything they have done.

Create a deadline for yourself and force yourself to hit the deadline - That is not helpful. At all.

Freewrite This is where you just write anything to do with anything. It is a good exercise but will not help writer's block for most authors.

Start another book - This is the path to the author's enemy... Abandoned stories. Most authors have a pile of unfinished stories in their files. Left to rot for no other reason than they started something else instead—Mostly because of writer's block!

The only thing you can really do—from my own experience and talking with other authors—and the only thing that will not stress you out or increase any anxiety is to break away from the story. But don't do nothing, like the *take a break* advice says. You need to get up and do something mundane to engage the autopilot part of your brain for a few hours. Personally, I drive for a long time. Hours if I have to. And I sing along with any music playing, and after a while, I start to think of the story that I'm stuck on. As the main part of your brain is busily focused on driving, I use a different part of my brain (I think I'm an author, not a scientist!), and somehow that works. At least to give me a way through, even if it's changing part of the plot or scrapping that chapter for something

else. Some people clean, some people exercise. It may not happen immediately, but focusing on autopilot really helps to break the analytical part of your brain away from the creative part. Allowing you to fix the story without anxiety mentally.

Imposter Syndrome

If you are an author and do not suffer from a degree of imposter syndrome on a regular basis, then you are in the minority. A minority so small it may be only you there, along with a few uber-successful authors that believe their own hype. Not trying to be insulting; I am jealous of you. But you are the exception, not the rule. Feel free to skip this part if this is you.

I am speaking to those who do feel the pangs of doubt.

The ones who feel alone.

The ones who feel that they are frauds.

The ones who feel that they are a failure.

The ones who feel that they are not good enough.

I am here to tell you that that is normal.

You are, most certainly, not alone.

When you are an artist and create something from your brain, you *will* doubt it. You will feel that it is not worthy of release. You will compare it to books you love and think yours is horrible.

When you feel all of this, do not worry. Even your favourite author will have felt it at some point. I have met many authors who are household names who *still* feel it with every release.

Imposter syndrome is most prevalent when someone has decided to become an author and is on the first steps to writing their story. They will wonder if they are good enough to call themselves authors. I am here to tell you... you are an author if you *say* you are one. You don't get magically bestowed that title when your first book is published. You can be an author and never publish at all. The imposter is in your mind only.

I suffer from imposter syndrome just after I release a book, just before any reviews come in. Not because I fear bad reviews—which I try to accept gracefully—but because the creating is over, and I doubt it was ready for release. The problem for me is that this never goes away. I never think a book I write is publishable. I have read reviews from people who adore my books. And I am so happy they do. But in my mind, I believe they are all laughing at me behind my back. I just have to ignore this and live my life.

So, your feelings are normal. You have to live with the doubt, as that will never go away. It just becomes more expected and thus less debilitating.

Drafting

I find the first draft the most fun part of the whole writing process. The messy, mistake-filled madness of that initial run-through. The result of countless coffees, mini breakdowns, self-doubt, writer's block, and fear.

The first draft is a life lived.

The first draft is proof that you could tell that story.

The first draft, no matter how many books you have already published, is an emotional one.

Christian Francis

The first draft is also terrible.

That's the horrible realisation every author will eventually come to.

When you are a new author, you will write that first draft thinking it is amazing. You will still be lost in the story you write, not looking at the writing itself. And when you eventually realise the truth of how many mistakes there are—not just in grammar but also in plot—it will be heartbreaking. Just rest assured, *all* first drafts suck.

When that first draft is done, no matter who you are or how many books you have written, you will sit back with a smug sense of accomplishment, not seeing that within those pages is a mess of terrible grammar, horrendous spelling, gaping plot holes, and mistakes that are so shocking, you will want to quit writing forever.

When I taught writing long, long ago, my students were aghast at the idea that books are not just written, sent off, and then published. They had a hard time appreciating that the author would have to redraft their book many times and send their manuscript off to proofreaders and editors.

I remember one of the students asking, "Why do you bother then? It sounds horrible." Oh, yes... It is. But it is also amazing.

After leaving your first draft to sit for a day, weeks, or however long you need a break, you will open up the first page and re-read your story.

You will hope it is a masterpiece.

Then you will read a scene and tut to yourself.

You know how to spell *from*. Yet all the way through your first chapter, it is spelt *form*.

You know what tense to write in, but this whole scene constantly switches between past and present tense.

Who the hell is Linda?! The main character is Sarah!

I could go on, and any author reading this will recognise these kinds of errors.

If you have had this happen and doubt yourself, DO NOT LOSE HEART!

Every author's first draft is a mess of mistakes and plotting mishaps. (Unless you are a robot who perfectly writes every time. In which case, why are you reading this book?) Your first draft was written with a mix of passion and doubt. Even with a perfectly mapped-out story, you will have rushed some parts and maybe planned out the scene wrong. Maybe underutilised a character. Perhaps not explained something right. And if you don't plan out your writing, plot strands may be left hanging. There may be inconsistencies.

This is normal. This is your first draft.

Think of the first draft as a sketch before you neaten up the lines.

The second draft will be where you bring it all together and fix those significant issues that you did not see in a 2 am writing binge.

In the third draft, you will mainly look at spelling and grammar.

Each author does different things on different drafts. But you *will* need to redraft.

Never believe your first or even second draft is the best it can be.

The worst part is that you will get to the point where you can't see the forest through the trees and are sick of the book. That is when you need a break from it before going back or need to send it to someone else to read.

One funny aside... I used to work for a famous author who wrote the roughest, most incomprehensibly terrible first-draft stories. But as they were already rich and famous, they got their staff to rewrite their drafts into coherent books for them, under the promise of money and CO-credit. A mammoth task but one the staff happily accepted. Then the author would (always, as this happened multiple times) send the finished manuscript to their publisher, take all the money and credit for themselves, and slander many other authors saying they were awful for using ghostwriters. I only tell this as evidence that the first draft is never perfect, no matter who you are.

And so you know, *all* mistakes can be fixed in the drafting process. No matter how big the plot hole. Never ditch a first draft. It is rough, but it can be fixed and polished to be what you want it to be.

Transitional scenes

Writing is a consuming task. It draws in the author more profoundly than it can draw in a reader, so much so that the author soon cannot see the scenes beyond their written words. The author can get lost in the plot and forget a simple key storytelling mechanic.

I have heard from authors, lost in their manuscripts, say that they dread the next transitional scene, as they either find them hard to keep engaging or get bored writing them. This isn't just a new author issue, but authors of all experience. When writing, it is easy for any author to forget that a book does not need to follow all the footsteps. When writing, going from A to B to C is logical and a clear pathway, but also totally unnecessary.

Even in the longest epic, you do not need to know how someone got somewhere if that journey has no consequence. Your story is not a minute-by-minute, blow-by-blow account of someone's experience (unless that's exactly what you are doing, then you can ignore this part, as it only applies to a standard fiction story.)

The reader only needs to read a transitional scene of someone going home if something of importance is revealed or if the scene is not a catalyst for a plot-based action.

Chapter breaks are your friend. They should be embraced, but for some reason, they are significantly underutilised in many books. A simple double return will put a space in a chapter, which serves as a time or location jump. When you do this, you are effectively changing the subject. Doing this is much less boring than writing an unneeded transitional scene. Remember, if it's boring for you to write, it will be just as boring to read.

There, see that? I have just written a chapter break. I have jumped ahead over many pages of convincing arguments and examples, and charts to the point where you all understand and agree with me on this subject.

The Narrator

So many rules regarding the narrator's voice are thrown about, but only one rule truly matters: Be consistent.

That's it.

Nothing else.

Standard narration is omniscient. Meaning not in or part of the story, just there telling the tale.

The usual tone for this omniscient narrator is formal. No colloquialisms. No swearing. No catchphrases. Nothing beyond what is either the Lee or the Dench. What is the Lee or the Dench? Well, that is one of the best ways I have found to write formal narration. If the narration is to be in a male voice, imagine Christopher Lee was narrating it. If a female, imagine Judy Dench... It can be anyone approximate to that class of person. It doesn't have to be English; it can be any nationality; ensure that they are 'proper' speakers. This helps you avoid having your narrator say something like, *'the day was as sweaty as a dog's asshole'*.

BUT

BUT

BUUUUT

This is only helpful if you *want* formal narration. You may want your narrator to have a personality, even if they are not a character in a book. You may want them to speak informally, swear etc., which is fine. It may not be standard to have an omniscient informal narrator, but it is your story to tell, so don't let anyone dictate rules just because of what is *normal*.

Here is where the consistency rule comes into play. If you choose one thing, stick to it. I have spoken to many authors who struggle with narration, and it is because they have not stuck to one style. Most had the most formal language for most of the story; then randomly, the narrator says something slang, swears or even states a personal opinion. Fixing that fixed the issues. Just choose a tack, and stick to it.

Consistency is the best way to be sure about your writing. If you are telling your story, be confident in doing so.

Your narrator can speak however you want, but you have to be concrete in your writing of them. You can even have multiple narrators; just be sure each has its own definite voice.

I suggest, and this is *only* a suggestion, but keep it formal if you are using an omniscient narrator. Mainly if the narrator is informal but not a real character in the book, it can confuse a story. The omniscient narrator's point is to tell a story in a nonintrusive way, allowing the character's personalities and dialogue to shine. The worst thing you can have is a narrator (that isn't a character in the book) being hilarious and charismatic, and the story's characters being not as interesting or fun to read.

The omniscient narrator is like the background of a painting. Important, but only there to set the scene.

Again... It is up to you. Just whatever you do, be sure of your path. Be consistent and unwavering.

There is an extra thing that some authors falter with. They give the narrator an opinion. And that opinion is preached. It's okay for a character to believe anything, and if your narrator is a character, then, of course, it's okay. Still, a third-person omniscient narrator who is not a character's voice should never have an opinion. This is because that opinion is presumed to be the author's and can be seen as preaching, which no fiction reader wants to endure, even if they agree with you.

Where to start and end

A concise but important section.... Many authors falter as they believe they *have* to know the ending to their story before they start their book.

Even for the plotters out there, *you do not need to know the end of a book to start it*. At all. Just because you don't know it right now means nothing. This should not dissuade you from starting in the slightest. You could plot the whole book to the end if you wanted to and figure the rest out later.

The same goes for *any* part of a book. Start, middle or end. You do not need to know those parts before starting your book. You can start writing scenes you *do* know first. You have to remember that writing is creation. It is not an exercise in planning. You can do it how you want; just don't let overthinking hold you back. If you only know a part of a book. Write that and see what happens.

But what happens if you start a book without an ending and can't complete it, or for whatever reason, you do not complete a story because of various missing parts? The best advice I can give you is never to give up on a book. *Ever.* That is not to say you must keep writing it until it's done. Just press pause and move on. Just because you can't or don't want to finish a book today does not mean you cannot do so tomorrow. Keep every single bit of writing you do. No exceptions. Keep it all.

I wish I had known this advice twenty years ago. I used to routinely delete stories that I gave up on. Stories I know now I could have looked at and reworked.

Even if you give up on writing, keep it all. Please. You never know if your path will return you to writing.

Writing for Market

A tricky subject and one that many writing classes try to make new authors focus on. Many writing books out there say you should write for market, as they consider it to be writing smarter, as your books will sell better. Guaranteed.

For those who don't know, writing for market is when an author is supposed to analyse current trends and look at the big sellers in your genre, then write a book to appeal to that audience, using the trends and styles of that moment in time.

Anyone who teaches this as a thing you must do to succeed is making the art of writing a soulless exercise. They are not teaching as they believe it, but to make more money themselves. They are not looking to help you. It is yet another absolutist rule that does not look at the facts:

- You cannot write a book for a trend with any guarantee that the trend will exist when you publish. Trends come and go faster than you can blink.
- If you don't believe in your writing, the readers won't either.

- Just because you *think* you know a trend, that you *think* you know something people love, if you don't love it, you will not be able to copy it for the market.
- No matter what your book or how based on market trends, is any guarantee that it will sell a single copy. No one can tell you otherwise.
- People are more likely to buy a book in their genre that excites them more than a clear rip-off of something else.
- You will not be the only person doing what you are doing, and market saturation will likely swallow your book into obscurity.

I am not saying you cannot make money writing for market. You 100% can. Many authors make a good living doing it. I do not see their method as anything good to teach as a rule to a newcomer. I personally see this method as having no creative merit. It's a business decision masked as creativity. Those authors *can* write. And they write fast. But they write for profit as their primary guide. I see nothing in this, for me anyway.

Getting new authors to do the same from the outset can ruin a burgeoning passion for the craft. Telling new authors this does nothing except make their writing journey a slog of corporate greed while removing all possible passion. Passion is what will

Anti Rule

teach them more. Passion will guide their journey. Getting new authors to write for market before they have even found their own writing voice is irresponsible. Sure, they may wish to do this later, but they should only try after they know their own style and voice.

Look at this in the light of films. You know when a movie gets successful and lots of rip-offs come out straight away? How many of those rip-offs are actually any good? None. They are all cash grabs, and evidently so. I have also read many books written for market—maybe hundreds. I have never read one that I consider a book I will ever read again. They are all disposable. They may sell, but that is not a sign of quality originality.

I have spoken to many authors who write for market who believe I am wrong and say they write quality and that they write differently than most other authors. They believe they have a more realistic mindset toward money and writing in modern times. But I say making money is not a sign that you are doing something right, and it is not realism that makes their money, but cynicism. The successful authors writing for market—and they are in the vast minority of ones that do—are also the same ones that have written *how-to* books about how to write for market and how to market your books. I have read those books too. They also always speak in absolutes, telling people they are wrong and that what they teach is the key to success. All of them negate the fact that they only got where they are through blind luck and not with any skill in analysis. It's like when people say Jeff Bezos is a self-made man, totally ignoring the fact that his start-up cash came from his wealthy parents. With anyone who tells authors that they have to write for market, each one of them ignores the fact that selling books of any kind is 98% luck and 1% skill, up until you get a following, then that percentage changes. And this doesn't change if you write for market or not.

With this subject, I leave it all up to you. This is my opinion, but whatever way you decide, do not believe anyone who says that is how you *need* to write your book. If you don't do so, you are stupid or destined to fail. It is *your* book to write. Do it how *you* want. If that ends up as writing for market, and that makes you happy, then awesome. Good on you. But for most, writing that way will never work out better than writing for yourself.

Writing for Market 2: Smaller Genre Marketability

Go into any bookshop; their main genre section is still just 'Fiction' as if all fiction books are the same. Then they may segregate the more niche categories into smaller sections—Like 'Sci-Fi & Fantasy' or 'Horror' (Not that many bookshops have a dedicated horror section anymore, and if they do, it's just shelves of Stephen King and other authors who are easy sellers.) Why do they not have proper genre definitions? It is quite a simple answer; It is not segregated anymore because sellers and publishers generally look down on anything that doesn't fit into their 'Fiction' category. They are not separating Sci-Fi & Fantasy because they want those books to be more accessible. They segregate them to get them away from the main fiction they prefer to promote.

You may think I am being paranoid in thinking this. If I am wrong, why do they not separate dramas, thrillers, and comedies? Like video stores used to do?

It's all because the big publishers *hate, hate, hate* books that do not fit their marketable 'fiction' banner because those genre books are aimed at a smaller audience—an audience who earns them less money. The audience for adult horror, fantasy, etc., is a small pool of wallets to aim at. Hence, many publishers won't even accept manuscripts from those genres. If it's YA sci-fi or YA horror, that is different, as YA is hot and profitable. But Adult? Nope. It's always down to the smaller imprints and indie publishing to push those genres to the max.

This segregation has meant that the literary agents representing those smaller genres are fewer. This truth is not meant to dissuade anyone from writing in one of those genres ; it is just a heads-up about the reality of the market. After all, you would not expect any agent to represent your book if you knew they could not sell it.

So, with all this in mind, what overall genre *should* you write in? That is a question many people who are starting to write ask me. If you are one of the lucky few that can write in any genre you want to, have a knowledge of each genre, and can get as much enjoyment with writing in all genres, then you are lucky. You can take a page out of the writing for market ideology and find a genre you could best succeed in—looking at market trends, analysing the audience, and crafting the book to hit all the sellable markers. Essentially you can aim your book for a bigger payback before constructing an outline.

There is little choice for the rest of us—the majority of us . We would never be able to write for market by choosing the best genre to sell to, as our writing is a passion for us, not a business model we can automate. We know the genres we are passionate about, and there is little way we could leave genres easily. So, those people who ask what genre to write in know what they would prefer; they just are unsure if it's a good idea.

There's the rub and the crux of the issue—People mix what they are writing for with what people want. This means they end up doubting what they *should* do. They hear many people out there telling them to analyse the market first. That they are stupid otherwise, then others say just write for passion. It's a lot of opposing voices screaming do this one thing, or you are wrong.

But in the end, it comes down to:

1. If you are writing for yourself because you feel a *need* to tell your story... you know what you will be doing. You know your genre. No matter what anyone says, you will end up writing what you love. You will hope it sells. You will hope people will love it. Nevertheless, you will write it anyway.
2. If you have a talent to write but don't care about what you write and just want to maximise your income, you could get a job as a copywriter or write to market.

Sure, you *could* write in a genre most open to success. But is that a path you want to take? Could you ignore the call of your author's passion in exchange for money? I find that the most challenging part of all of this. For me, writing is about my personal craving to tell my stories. Even this book you are reading now is not a cash grab as other such books may be. It's not to make money. It was born out of my need to speak the truth about writing after seeing so many lies out there. It's why this book is small—as the messages are simple. It's why it's cheap—It's not for profit. It's why it's written informally—To be easily understood. There is nothing cynical about this book. I did not even plan to write it. I did not think, 'Ah, *there is a market for writing books*'. I even stopped halfway through my next novel to write this, as I felt an undeniable craving to do so. And that is how 99% of authors regard their writing. They will write *when* they need to write. They will write *what* they need to write. The whole idea of choosing a genre for success would be abhorrent to most authors, simply for the fact that writing for them is a calling, not a choice.

Some positivity...

There are so many tips and rules you should never follow, which begs the question, is there any good writing advice out there? Most definitely! But it's not always about the written word. Here I will pick out the best quotes of advice for new authors. These are ones that I believe can help and inspire you, not insult and restrict, as so many 'rules' and 'tips' do. These are words of wisdom that should be taught to all aspiring authors. (Please note, not all of these people have 100% great advice all the time, these are just the best bits) – I have also included my comments on them.

***"You might be writing rubbish, but you can always go back over it and make it a better read"* – James Herbert**

First. Drafts. Always. Suck.

***"Take it a page at a time"* – John Steinbeck**

It's not a race.

"Do mindless tasks while thinking" – Chuck Palahniuk

Note- this is the best way to work out plot issues!

"First, find out what your hero wants, then just follow them!" – Ray Bradbury

Advocating the panster method, but still great advice for all authors.

"Start as close to the end as possible" – Kurt Vonnegut

It's the best way to ensure your story is as enthralling as possible.

"Do back exercises. Pain is distracting" – Margaret Atwood

Oh, I wish I had known this before I started!

"Remember why you write" – Stephen King

Authors often forget and start to believe that it is for any other reason than a need to create stories.

"If there's a book that you want to read, but it hasn't been written yet, then you must write it" – Toni Morrison

It sounds obvious, but it is the best way to decide on a story.

"If you're using dialogue, say it aloud as you write it. Only then will it have the sound of speech" – **John Steinbeck**

And avoids errors!

"Employ an unreliable narrator, preferably one who doesn't know he is insane and has no recollection of such events as digging into a grave to rip out the teeth of his recently departed lover" – **Edgar Allen Poe**

A great bit of advice for anyone using first-person narration. Not all narrators need to know it all. It's better if they don't, at least if they don't say they do.

"Don't be nervous. Work calmly, joyously, recklessly on whatever is in hand" – **Henry Miller**

Try to never lose the joy of writing

"Be your own editor/critic. Sympathetic but merciless!" – **Joyce Carol Oates**

Better you than someone else, at least on the second draft

"Work stories out in your head when you can't write" – **Alice Munro**

Daydreaming the story can take you to places you never thought you would go!

***"Just do what feels true to you. Speak your heart, however strange or revelatory it is. Don't be ashamed of how your imagination works. What a reader wants to discover in a book is what you hold uniquely in your head"* – Clive Barker**

Yes! Create your own art. Write for yourself.

***"You can only write regularly if you're willing to write badly... Accept bad writing as a way of priming the pump, a warm-up exercise that allows you to write well"* – Jennifer Egan**

Accept that not everything will be great!

***"Writing anything is better than nothing"* – Katherine Mansfield**

Even the worst writing can have a jewel of an idea in it!

***"Grab 'em by the throat and never let 'em go"* – Billie Wilder**

Remember, you are writing a story, not a play-by-play. It is supposed to be enthralling. Cut needless transitional scenes if the plot seems too slow to you!

"Increase your word power. Words are the raw material of our craft. The greater your vocabulary the more effective your writing. We who write in English are

Anti Rule

***fortunate to have the richest and most versatile language in the world. Respect it"* – PD James**

Words are your friend

***"Perfection is like chasing the horizon. Keep moving"* – Neil Gaiman**

Stop worrying about a book when it's out. Onto the next!

***"Don't worry about the bad drafts"* – Miranda July**

This advice has been mentioned many times in this book but bears repeating.

***"You have to get to a very quiet place inside yourself. And that doesn't mean that you can't have noise outside. I know some people who put jazz on, loudly, to write. I think each author has her or his secret path to the muse"* – Maya Angelou**

No author writes the same. There are no rules as to when and how you write.

"Read, read, read. Read everything - trash, classics, good and bad, and see how they do it. Just like a carpenter who works as an apprentice and studies the master. Read! You'll absorb it. Then write. If it's good, you'll find out. If it's

not, throw it out of the window" – **William Faulkner**

Even the worst books can teach you something.

"Ignore all proffered rules and create your own, suitable for what you want to say" – **Michael Moorcock**

REBEL. REBEL. REBEL!

"Put it aside. Read it pretending you've never read it before. Show it to friends whose opinion you respect and who like the kind of thing that this is" – **Neil Gaiman**

Simple, practical advice.

"Don't obsess about genres" – **Stephen King**

YES! So many authors restrict themselves by worrying about what genre they think they should write.

"Write what you need to write, not what is currently popular or what you think will sell" – **PD James**

Writing should always be a passion, not a business decision.

"There's no free lunch. Writing is work. It's also gambling. You don't get a pension

plan. Other people can help you a bit, but —essentially you're on your own. Nobody is making you do this: you chose it, so don't whine" – **Margaret Atwood**

Reality is harsh.

"The main rule of writing is that if you do it with enough assurance and confidence, you're allowed to do whatever you like. (That may be a rule for life as well as for writing. But it's definitely true for writing.) So write your story as it needs to be written. Write it honestly, and tell it as best you can. I'm not sure that there are any other rules. Not ones that matter" – **Neil Gaiman**

Probably the best advice you will ever read.

About all the 'rules'

Why is it that people declare rules as if writing is something that needs to be consistent across all authors and genres? What is it that people teaching these things are doing that they cannot see an error in what they teach? It cannot be intentional. Or can it?

It can.

It is.

It is entirely intentional.

It is not malicious, though.

It is just a difference in how they view writing.

All those teaching these 'rules' and 'tips' approach writing as the old publishers did; They want uniformity across books. They want *all* books to read the same. They want *all* books to be as easily digestible as possible so that a reader can absorb the plot most quickly and simply.

That is the issue.

They see that as a good thing.

It is not.

It is the murder of writing.

It is the slaughter of the author's original voice.

It is the damning of an art form that craves to be brave.

This is why new authors need help with all this advice. New authors come to the fold with ideas that are bursting to break forth. Stories filled with their own passion and emotions. Tales that feel like they will make the author explode if they do not write it down. These new authors look for guidance but are instead met with a wall of counterproductive rules damaging to the creation of written art.

Anti Rule

The rules are not there to help.

They are there to homogenise.

They are there to strip an author's voice and culture and only leave the plot. That, to me, is a travesty.

I don't want to read something not in an original voice. I don't want to read something similar to the last book I read. I want to read a story in the voice of someone from a different generation and culture. I want the words before me to brim with the author's style. I don't want it to be easy.

Here is the issue summed up as best I can: You are a human. You have a human voice. Your human voice is individual. When you write, your voice becomes your own words. These words present the plot. Like storytellers of old, as they sat at a campfire, regaling people with tales of wonder and enchantment. The storyteller's personality was an intrinsic part of that story. Just as your writing shows your personality. The way your voice is written is uniquely yours.

The rules *hate* the storyteller aspect. They want the story, but they want a robot to read it in its most basic and quick form. They want everything to be consistent and every voice to be the same.

This book you are reading is to deter you from becoming that robot.

No one can force you to change anything. It is your story. Unless it's spelling, grammar, plot hole or story error, anything you are told to do is yours to ignore. You are not beholden to these rules. Sure, if you have a publisher, they may insist on this. But know that this is not the *only* way.

You just need to remember that your writing needs to breathe, not be strangled, and the 'rules' and 'tips' mostly hold onto your windpipe with an iron grip. Being a writer is not education, it is not a textbook. It is art. When faced with the choice to follow any of these rules, no matter what I or anyone else says or recommends, it is *your* choice. You may want to edit your writing to follow all the rules. They all may speak to you, and you may agree with each and every one. That is fine. Follow your heart. Do as you feel you need to. Just never forget... Your art is yours.

Your art is yours.

Your art is yours.

Your art is yours.

Your art is yours.

Your art is yours.

What comes next...

You have written your manuscript... What next?...

Editing

I don't care who you are; your book needs editing. But that does not have to be a ludicrously awful proposition. You just have to know what options are available to you.

Firstly remember that if you use any kind of editor, they might not be the editor for you. An editor is like a partner; not just anyone will suffice, and their opinions may be contrary to what you believe, so shop around if you are looking for one. You can even ask an editor to edit a sample page to see how they edit. Don't be afraid to ask questions. You also need to look at what *kind* of editing you need, for there are many kinds... Proofreader – Someone who looks for spelling and grammar errors in your text.

Copy / Line Editor – More in-depth than copy editing, as they will also look at word choice, style, sentence structure and consistency line by line for a better flow.

Developmental Editor – Someone who looks at the story as a whole and suggests where you may need to expand, improve, or change the content for your book to become the best it can be.

Structural Editor – Will look at the book's overall structure and content of your book but, unlike a developmental editor, the structural editor will, more often than not, makes any changes themselves.

Editors typically offer all or some of these options for authors to choose from. Each has a different price depending on the time needed to devote to it; they may even provide a hybrid edit for precisely what you are looking for. (As a side note, they also may name these editing types differently from how I labelled them above, so make sure to ask what each involves). Personally, I only want my books to be proofread and then copy/line edited. I have no interest in anyone telling me how to improve my story – but that's just me. You need only to do as much as you are comfortable doing .

Many authors get overexcited to get their manuscript sent off for editing as soon as possible, but this can be a mistake, as it can make the editing process drawn out and a very painful process. Please, try not to do this. You need to ensure the manuscript is near the finish line, as you can get it before any editor gets involved. To do that, you will need to self-edit first. And this process may be time-consuming, but boy, is it needed.

The first step to self-editing is to redraft the script yet again, but only look for errors in your writing. Sure, you may have done it once, but do it again and again.

The next step of self-editing is to hear your book back to you. The easiest way to do that is to record yourself narrating it section by section, then listen to it back. Alternatively, if you have dyslexia or sight issues, or just can't be bothered, you can throw the manuscript into an online text-to-voice reader. I cannot stress how important this whole step is. You may have silently read the book a thousand times to yourself or even read it aloud, but trust me when I say you will have missed so many mistakes. *Hearing* it spoken back to you will illuminate so many more errors in your writing: all that bad spelling, the jumbled sentences, the continuity errors.

Sure, these two steps may be an annoyance and almost impossible to endure, but both will find things you need to fix. But the harsh truth is that no matter how many errors you find or how many times you edit, an editor will find more. And an even harsher truth... No matter how many people check it, spelling and grammar errors will *always* slip through the net.

You will be stuck editing everything if you have zero budget and cannot afford an editor. But that is not an impossible task—just a time-consuming one. In addition to the above two steps, a wealth of resources online are available to help you (though each will be time-consuming and boring as hell). Writing software like *Grammarly* or *Pro Writing Aid* offers free trials to error-correct small bits of text at a time, so use them. Put your manuscript in a few pages at a time. Feel free to ignore their passive voice warnings, but they could flag errors you haven't caught and offer some limited suggestions on sentence structure you may wish to follow. MS Word should also be used in addition to them, as it has a fantastic spelling checker that is better than most others.

When it comes down to it, if you are only editing yourself, without a professional, then you need to use every free tool you can, but when you have exhausted those avenues, all that is left is to find a beta reader. Maybe it's a friend or family member; perhaps you have someone online willing to do you a favour. Never be afraid to ask, and never be upset if people don't or can't help.

And if you *do* get an editor, or a beta reader, please remember to take all they say lightly. Unless it's a correction due to an actual error, all they offer is merely an opinion, and you do not have to follow it if you don't want to. It is *your* story; you are the only person who can say what should be included. If it's a suggestion that something may read better another way, balance the feedback's pros and cons, and do what *you* feel is best.

What kind of publisher?

I'm sure you started your writing journey dreaming that your book will be one day in a bidding war between the big publishers, then you will sign a multi-book deal and be paid a lot of money. After that, the movie adaptations and fame await!

Of course, that is a dream. The reality is way more depressing.

You have three routes ahead of you... Self-publishing, indie publishing, or 'traditional' publishing. Each of them has pros and cons. I have dealt with all three publishing types, and I chose self-publishing as it gives me the most control over my product.

This is a huge subject, so I will try to be as concise as I can:

Traditional Publishers.

I hate that term. *Traditional*. Urgh. Anyway, it is when a publisher buys the publishing rights to your book, have you sign a contract, and (mostly) pays you an advance. But unlike other publishers, their books are pre-printed, warehoused in batches, and sold via sale or return to bookstores etc. Think Random House, Harper Collins, Penguin etc.

Everyone dreams of being signed by one of these, but it is not the dream you think it is. Yes, you could get paid a huge advance for a multi-book deal! They could pay you £100,000 for that! Amazing right? No. It actually isn't. As they do not pay this in one sum. They usually pay larger sums over a period (on average) of five years. Meaning you would get £20,000 a year for that £100,000 advance. Which is less than the minimum wage for anyone over 21 in the UK. And this is *only* an advance on money still to be earned. This means you won't make a penny more until the publisher has earned back your advance. (Hence why it is called an advance.) And with book sales not being what they once were and bookstores disappearing daily, this could end with you never getting a penny more and your publisher dropping you.

The traditional publishing world is also heartless and cares not for art or the author's voices. All the rules that you read me argue earlier on? They believe in them. And their editors are there to ensure that you follow those rules. The contract will give the publisher full ownership of everything they put out there. So unless a book matches their vision, they will not print it. You will have no power over anything unless you become a big seller for them. Then the dynamic can change.

Most authors I know, some of whom were once very famous, have since left traditional publishers, as the publisher demands ruined their love of the art. As it did mine. (Though I was never famous).

When someone asks me, I say good luck but remember to be very open-eyed about it all. It's run like a business. They may woo you in the door but treat you like a product when you sign that contract —a product they only want to deal with when you make them money.

Indie publishers

The middle ground, and akin to the rebel alliance against the traditional publisher's empire. There are two kinds of indie publishers, ones who do the same as traditional publishers but do so on a much smaller scale and are more like boutique traditional publishers, and come with the same pros and cons as their big brothers (hence why I won't be discussing them in this section). I am talking about the more common, smaller companies that were born out of necessity as the traditional publishers refused to keep up with the emerging digital world. (for which they still lag quite a way behind). These indie publishers will still sign a contract with you but will work on a profit-share basis. Nothing upfront, but you will earn a small amount of money as soon as the book is sold.

These publishers also almost entirely exist on a print-on-demand (POD) model. Unlike the traditional and boutique traditional publishers who have their books printed and warehoused, these publishers work through POD platforms like Amazon or IngramSpark to get the books out there.

There are issues with indie publishers, and they are issues that can be significant. Most do not have the marketing reach to make an author a lot of money as traditional publishers could. Nor do they have the business acumen to grow beyond a certain point. Some may be awesome people and have tens of thousands of followers on social media, as well as a lot on their newsletter subscription, but that is all they have. They will almost always be segregated by genre and plumbed only into that genre's audience, which means that the sales will never be of a level that could make anyone really rich.

Following a POD model also means that most bookshops will not stock their books, as most bookshops, etc., require a sale or return policy, which you should not do on a POD platform as you are taking on a significant risk. Sale or return is fine for a company with a lot of money, but for an indie publisher, an influx of returns from bookshops could bankrupt them, so they stick by and large to a standard 'order and keep' model of publishing.

Because of this and the traditional publisher's grip on the non-digital bookselling world, indie publishers find themselves making their niche online and at conventions and fairs, happy that they are not the soulless business machines that they may see traditional publishers as. These indie publishers are also only staffed by a few people, not a large office or workers, but that is not a bad thing.

In fact, the downsides I have said above are not really a downside when you consider the pros. What they lack in reach and money, they make up for in passion. They make up for in a want to work *with* an author. To form strong relationships with their authors and cement a future with them. They are not there for an immediate return under threat of being ditched—And that is a beautiful thing. When you find an indie publisher that is part of your 'tribe', the cons to their business fade into the distance.

Of course, no indie publisher is the same, and like with any business, there are bad ones out there too. Ones that are only out to make money and have zero care for the author. Here are a few signs of a bad or amateur indie publisher to look out for:

- If they ask for any money from you. You should not pay a thing. Not even a small amount. Not for editing, marketing, or anything. The publisher's role is to do this

for you, not to charge you for the service. You created the art. That's your part of everything done.
- Vanity publishers. These are publishers who charge you upfront to publish anything you wish. No vanity publisher is held in high regard. Your name will be tarnished if you do that.
- If they do not offer you a professional editing service free of charge.
- If they do not offer you a quality book cover service free of charge. One which is also transparent with fonts and images (more on this later.)
- If they do not offer you dedicated company-registered ISBNs. Any company using free ISBNs from Createspace, Amazon or Ingram are people who have no care for their business or for you.
- If they are not transparent with their payment schedule and have it clearly explained in their contract.
- If they have no social reach or marketing strategy that will benefit you or is much more than you can do yourself.
- If they have any bad history. Check online. Research. Ask around. Find out other opinions. You don't want your art tied to bad people.

Self-publishers

Also known as doing it all yourself.

This is hard and can cost, but it is the option with the most control.

Of course, this would mean you have to edit, design, publish and market off your own back, which is no easy task. This is why indie publishers can be a blessing. Though if you *can* do all that yourself, then you do not need a publisher at all.

The learning curve is steep, and the minus is that it will cost you, if not in money, then insanity. The hardest part of it is the marketing, as you are marketing your book, and *yourself*. Your brand. And that is not for everyone. If you are the kind of person that needs professional support, then self-publishing may not be for you at all.

For those interested, I have added a self-publisher section in this book to try and dispel some myths and help you along your journey.

Literary agent or no literary agent

If you want to go the traditional publishing route, you may need a literary agent. But not always. Sure, an agent can navigate the process of getting your book signed by a big publisher, but nowadays, there are many routes to that by yourself.

Christian Francis

What are the advantages of getting an agent?

- They know the processes well.
- Their reputation can ease the process of getting noticed.
- They are experienced in aspects you have no idea about.
- They have established connections in the publishing world.
- They will fight your corner, as they get a percentage of your earnings, which is in their best interests.
- But for every pro, there is always a con,
- They may not be reputable, and you may be conned. Not all agents are good.
- They traditionally take 15% of earnings, which is a huge chunk.
- It takes a long time to get published like this.
- They may not have expertise in your genre, or it may not be the genre in fashion, making their job impossible as they won't have the right contacts.
- They will not waste their time if they cannot sell your work, and you will be back to square one.
- They are not there to make sure your artistic vision is honoured. They are there to get you, and them, money.

Personally, I would rather punch myself in the face than do this again. Besides, even *if* you are successful in getting an agent, you then have to endure a lengthy process of finding appropriate publishers, querying them, pitching them, contract negotiation... It's not a fun thing to do. But sometimes you can circumvent the agent and query directly to the publisher yourself...

Queries and rejections

I have no idea how people can send out queries, whether to publishers or agents.

(The process to both is more or less the same.)

I hate it all. Not because of some issues I have with the process, just... It's... It's heartbreaking and anxiety educing; frankly, I can no longer stand it. Keep in mind that 99.99% of queries *will* get rejected. And that rejection hurts. Each and every time.

You may get a rejection in the form of a standard email saying no thank you and wishing you well but without any personalisation or any trace of humanity. It is cold and makes you feel like you have wasted your time.

You may never get a reply, and the unknown is always horrible. You will be stuck thinking *Should I resubmit? What if they never got the book in the first place?*

A personalised rejection. A letter stating exactly why your book is rejected. These are awful as they are still rejections, but they cushion the blow. Most will say things like it is not for them because of A, B and C, but they wish you well.

You may get rejected but asked to submit another book should you have one and if you wish to try again.

I can offer no advice for this part of the process as it's more or less unavoidable. If you submit a query, it will most likely get rejected. And most of the time, it's not due to the quality of the book. It might be because they do not want another book of that genre/subject. It might be that they are currently not looking to pick up authors like you. It might be that they are too busy, so they blanket reject many books. It might be one of a bazillion reasons aside from what your book is like. But it also could be because they just don't like your writing and do not wish to go further.

It's a challenging and painful process, but one that has been pushed aside with the accessibility of self-publishing. As soon as I could, I stopped ever getting involved in this process because life is too short to actively engage in anything that leads to heartbreak and anxiety!

Of course, if you get a rejection letter with reasons why, you may look at that as constructive criticism and want to rewrite your work based on that. But should you? That's up to you. If you connect with the feedback and see its value, then, of course, a rewrite may be what is needed, but their opinion is just that; opinion. They are not right or wrong (Unless they are pointing out actual mistakes), so like a review, you can choose how you engage with it.

Self-Publishing Pointers

If, after reading this book, you think that you may want to go the self-publishing route, or maybe you are trying to navigate it at the moment, here are some bits I think may help. Things that no one talks about!

eBooks - To flow or be fixed?

People need to be made aware of one main fact about eBooks; People can (and regularly do) choose their own font and font size. Whether changed to a more dyslexia-friendly font, or another accessible font for those with sight issues, any formatting you give no option to change could cost you sales.

For print, the font choice, font size, and layout of each page can be whatever you want it to be. It is printed and fixed. But eBooks are not, or more specifically, *should* not be. Of course, you *can* choose to publish your eBook as a fixed format and with all fonts determined so it reads more like a pdf. Doing this will stop some people from buying your book. If they have sight or reading issues and cannot amend the text to set it to how they need it, they will simply not buy that book.

You *need* your eBook to be reflowable to be accessible to all. This simply means that your book's content can be adjusted in its orientation to fit the size of the screen reader and whose fonts can be adjusted. Doing this will ensure that more people can buy and read your book. Don't be foolish and cut your audience down just for the sake of some notion that your text *has* to be in a certain way—that is what your print editions are for.

Book Covers

When an author has an idea for a cover, they may wish to enlist the services of an artist or designer. If they do this, they need to ensure they have *some* idea of what you want, along with—if possible—comparative examples for tone etc. But they should not ask for anything *too* exact as the cover will be better served if there is room for artist interpretation/experience. Remember, they are using an artist here, and the author is not the artist, so what they ask for may not 100% work. Use the artist's experience, so they can make something you may not have expected that may be a lot more commercially viable. Rely on their skills!

Whether you use an artist or make your own covers, DO NOT USE AI ART. AI art is made up of parts of stolen images from other artists. The AI image bank is, more often than not, crawled from Google without licensing the imagery used. It is not for commercial use. Adobe's new AI library is allegedly based on images they own in their libraries, but I will believe that when I see it!

It is hilarious when you go into a bricks and mortar bookshop and look at the fiction title for thrillers. They can be generally lumped into three cover categories:

- Silhouette(s)
- Building and Silhouette(s)
- Bold with a contrasted murder weapon (rope, gun, knife etc)

The major publishers don't even try to make their books stand out or look interesting. So when you have a cover you need to make, you have to ensure you do what they do. Research the genre's covers. Then look to get a cover made that will stand out from them, not blend in. If you are writing horror and all the current, comparable books out there are all dark and murky, make your cover bright and colourful. Keep in mind that most people only see that cover for a split second, (whether scrolling or in a bookshop), so you only have a millisecond to grab them with it. Remember readers *do* judge books by their covers!

Then if your cover does grab them, the next important thing is the book's title...

Licenses

With any cover creation, you must ensure you have licenses for any imagery and fonts used. Images and fonts were created by someone somewhere, and they make a living making that art, so their products are not for you to steal.

Most fonts are free for personal use but also likely require a license for commercial usage. Usually, there are different tiers for eBook, print, video etc… and it can get quite expensive. With that in mind, using a free commercial font is best if you are on a budget. (Big font libraries such as Adobe are all free for commercial use)

Additionally, you will need to ask any cover designer you use to provide licence information for any stock imagery and fonts they may have used. I have seen dozens of published books use stock images as part of the design, and those images are used without a license.

Be kind to the artists and pay for a license if you use their work.

Book Titles

Learn from my mistake. The title is so very important.

It really needs to be original and has not been used widely before.

My first novel is called *'Everyday Monsters'*. That is a *perfect* title for it. I was so happy with that title. After the book came out, I soon discovered that people mistook it for other books of the same name. I had not researched the title, and because of this, it affected the sales of my book significantly. A couple of months later, I added a suffix of *'The Animus Chronicles Book 1'* to the book, which helped, but by then, it was too little too late.

When it comes down to it, your book has to be first on the list when searching online. You cannot expect anyone to remember your name, so it has to be a title unlike others or at least different enough for database algorithms to find yours and find it easily.

This is why one of my books is called *"The Sacrifice of Anton Stacey"*. It includes a character name which is not a used name in books, and the title is emotive enough to be intriguing to a buyer. When you search for it, even if spelt wrong, it appears first on all searches online. That is what you want. That is the aim.

Even if that one title you have is perfect, even if you love it, look for others called it. If it isn't the only one, I strongly urge you to find another title!

Pull quotes

A pull quote is a quote from someone saying how great the book is that appears on the book cover. (Some people also call them blurbs, though others call the book synopsis a blurb. Terminology is all over the place in book publishing!)

A fact – Potential readers don't care if someone who is not a household name loves your book.

Sorry.

It is the truth.

Putting a pull quote on the cover from someone your customers do not know is a waste of space. In fact, it can work against you. If the pull quote is awesome and they look closely, and it's from a random blog reviewer, this could cause the customer to move on to another book, as they may see it as a sign of lesser quality as there it is not a known, reputable source.

I wish it weren't so, but it is.

Though a hypocrite, I have put on pull quotes from non-famous people on my books.

Why would I do that? I know it can work against the book sales, right?

Because I know the facts already, and I don't care if it affects sales. With all these bits of advice, you don't *have* to follow them. I am just putting the facts out there, and you can do as you please with it. For pull quotes, if a potential buyer looks at the quote on the cover and moves on because the pull quote is not from a good enough source, then I do not want them as a customer. I don't care if they don't ever read my work.

For me, this fact does not deter me from not following it. It may be to you ; hence me putting it out there.

Blurbs

Different people have different terms for this. Some call it a summary, some a synopsis, some a blurb. I call it a summary (as to me, a blurb is the pull quote, but that's neither here nor there), So I will use the popular terminology of *blurb* for this section. I am talking about the paragraph description of the book that appears on the back cover and the online product listing pages.

This blurb is so very important. You know that. Everyone does. But I have discovered a sad fact: Many authors cannot write an intriguing synopsis to save their lives. They may be fantastic fiction authors, but when it comes to blurbs, most indie authors seem to leave all skill at the door and write something that sells nothing.

Do not think I am being cruel here. This is not the author's fault. Blurb writing is a totally different skill set from fiction writing. It's something most authors would not even think about researching.

Here are some key pointers to help with blurb writing, but it is different for some books, so take these points as guides, not rules.

- The blurb is essentially a film trailer in writing form to market your book. Treat it as such. It is to grab and make a potential reader curious to read more.
- Try to keep the word length between 500—800 words. Any more can be off-putting for a potential customer to read, and less than that can sometimes seem not persuasive enough.
- Start with the whole premise as a single pitch line. The vaguer and more trailer-like, the better. It should be a pitch line to grab people. For Peter Benchley's *Jaws*,

the publisher used *'One man against a giant killer shark and a town that won't face the truth'*. There is nothing wrong with this, per se, but it's very dull. It would be better if it were something like, *'If you want to survive, do not go into the water.'* This would be in bold above the rest of the blurb, which should be...
- A no-spoiler overview of the plot set-up. You do not need to talk about all the characters, subplots or anything non-plot related. Just the main brush strokes to make people want to know more.
- Tense can be anything, though most write this in the present tense, even if the book is not.

With the advent of ChatGPT, I would (surprisingly) recommend that technology to help you with this. First, write the synopsis yourself—about 300 words—then put it into ChatGPT and ask it to rewrite to be more of a sales pitch, as well as more enticing to customers. This kind of usage is not long enough in word count or used in an arena where it could use plagiarised content, but if worried, there are sites online that you can put your text into to check for plagiarism. NEVER—and I cannot stress this enough—never use AI to write your prose. Helping with sales pitches is fine, but prose makes the book not *yours*, and using AI for that would most likely use someone else's published words, and would have a case for plagiarism.

Going Wide

Going wide, simply put, is when you get your book released onto as many digital and print platforms as possible. You may wish to sign up to IngramSpark, Smashwords, or one of the billion other third-party distributors, but even the best of them are restricted to places they can sell to. For example, virtually no third-party platform will supply to Google Play (even though some *still* say they do) as Google changed their terms and conditions, so only the publisher or author can upload an eBook or audiobook to sell through them.

When you want your book to be accessible to all, and to be easily ordered by all bookshops and libraries, then you have to look into the gaps that your distributor has and fill them yourself. Do not let this discourage you. Getting your books out there is a simple process; the difficult part is finding the places you need to upload to.

But, if you have your book up on Kindle Unlimited (for eBook) or KDP Expanded

Distribution (for Print), then you cannot put your books *anywhere* else that Amazon doesn't supply to, as these are exclusive sales channels. No other platform demands exclusivity as Amazon does, so don't feel pressured into signing up to them. You can simply sell your eBook on standard KDP or your print book on Amazon sales only and leave the expanded distribution to another provider. But you may not care about your book being everywhere and be quite happy just being on Amazon, and that is fine.

Neither is a wrong way.

Personally, I sell on KDP only to Amazon, not using Kindle Unlimited or

Expanded Distribution. I then use IngramSpark for most other places, except for Google Play which I upload separately to. But this is just me. You may find a better route that works for you. Just don't go in blind—research, research, research.

KDP vs Ingram vs Createspace vs Draft2Digital vs vs vs vs

I will say this right away – *No company is the best company*. No matter what anyone tries to tell you. Each has positives and negatives.

Amazon KDP

PROS

- Easy to use
- Access to the most significant single-book market
- Free to use
- Free ISBNs for all customers
- Cheap print costs

CONS

- ISBNs are exclusive only to Amazon and cannot be used elsewhere.
- Going with Kindle Unlimited is exclusive, so you can't sell on any other platform, essentially ignoring a large section of your potential audience.
- Their expanded distribution for print books is woeful and does not distribute that wide.
- Amazon carries a lot of stigma, meaning that many people, including most booksellers, refuse to buy there.
- Amazon routinely cancel accounts for no reason. There are horror stories of authors having books or accounts taken down, and the customer support is so terrible that it is a losing battle to get anything back. You don't even have to do anything wrong for them to cancel your account.
- Kindle Unlimited exclusivity has a clause in the contract that they will cancel your

account if you release a book anywhere else. There are stories of authors' books being pirated and illegally leaked, which KDP then found on an automated web crawl. Because of this, they cancelled the author's account for breaking exclusivity terms—despite the book being pirated without permission. Getting the account back for this is a losing battle as well. Amazon may be cheap and convenient, but they treat authors horribly, and their customer support is one of the worst I have ever experienced.
- The quality of print books is not great compared to others.

IngramSpark

PROS

- Excellent print quality (for the most part, they can sometimes be inconstant, more often than not, though they are way better than Amazon.)
- They offer a Groundwood paper option.
- A wide distribution model for print and digital. You could list with them alone, and your book will be accessible to 99% of outlets and platforms.
- Free to list

- Free ISBNs (US customers only)
- No exclusivity clause

CONS

- Horrible non-user friendly website
- No free ISBNs to non-US customers
- They lie and say they distribute to Google Play when in fact, they do not. Well, they *do* send the books, but Google Play only allows the publisher or author to release them on their platform.
- They take a percentage of all expanded distribution sales, which is terrible for anyone with a best-selling book.

I could go through all the platforms, but as you see, even the two biggest ones I mentioned have equal bad and good. It's just a question about which platform you feel most comfortable using. Many people swear by one platform, but your experience may differ. Look at each of the platforms carefully. Look at customer feedback. All you can do is try it out for yourself! Besides, you can always change the platform at a later date!

As mentioned, I release my books on KDP but do not choose Kindle Unlimited or Expanded Distribution. I use IngramSpark for paperback, eBook, and jacketed hardcover for distributing wide

(KDP do not provide jacketed hardcovers). I also sell my eBooks direct on Google Play. I also put my audiobooks on Audible. I believe all of this gives my book an extensive reach (aside from the audiobooks, which *could* be on more platforms if I went non-exclusive on Audible.)

Paper

As mentioned as a pro point for Ingram in the previous section, they give the paper option of Groundwood which few other POD services do. Most just provide cream or white paper types.

I must stress that nothing is wrong with standard cream or white paper printing. I just personally prefer Groundwood for my fiction. It is an eggshell paper type, meaning it has a slight texture to it and resembles a more mass-market book paper, as used by book printers before digital print came along. I feel that it gives the text more of a weathered feel, and really enhances your story to the reader.

Either way, you choose, there is no wrong choice. It's all about personal preference.

ISBNs

International Standard Book Numbers (ISBN) are the numeric identifiers of book entries within the

Christian Francis

ISBN databases that all book buyers have access to, as well that it feeds information to point-of-sale scanners to give limited information like the book's price and title etc., The ISBN information is all the metadata of the book. It includes not only the title, author, and price - but the synopsis, keyword tags, categories, front cover art, physical info about that edition (trim size, cover type, page count), and most importantly, the publisher name.

All ISBNs are assigned to a publisher name, not an individual name. Meaning if you buy some yourself, then they need to be registered under a publisher's name. And if you buy a cheap ISBN from a non-registered ISBN seller, then the publisher will be listed as them.

All ISBNs are individual to all print editions of books and audiobooks (eBooks don't require them to be sold on many platforms, and audiobooks don't need them on Audible). Each country has its own official ISBN seller. For example, it is Bowker in the UK, Thorpe-Bowker in Australia, and Nielsen in the UK.

The question is, does a self-published author need to buy their own ISBN? That depends. If you are happy just selling on Amazon and not caring who is listed as the publisher, then you can use KDPs free ISBNs. But they can only be used on Amazon, and you cannot use the free ISBN elsewhere. This is the same for the free ISBNs from Createspace and

Anti Rule

IngramSpark (US only). All these platforms give free ISBNs just for their selling platform and wide distribution.

If you want to go wider with your book and sell in all the places you can, you will need to buy your own ISBN. If you don't care who is listed as the publisher, many third-party ISBN sellers exist. Companies who resell them cheap, but their company name will be listed as the publisher on all metadata records.

If, like me, you care who is down as publisher, then you will need to buy your own from a registered seller, and it depends where you live as to what it will cost. Currently (June 2023) ISBNs cost:

For 1 ISBN

- UK £91
- US $125
- AU $44AUD

For 10 ISBNs

- UK £174
- US $295
- AU $88AUD

For 100 ISBNs

- UK £379

- US $575
- AU $480AUD

For 1000 ISBNs

- UK £979
- US $1,500
- AU $,3035AUD

As you see, it is quite expensive.... Unless you live in Canada, New Zealand or Denmark. Then you can get them *free* from their government! (I'm sure there are other amazing countries that also do the same). It is pretty cost prohibitive for the rest of us, so you need to weigh up if you need them.

When you buy your own ISBN, you will be able to use that ISBN across all platforms for each edition of the book. The paperback for your book will have the same ISBN no matter where it is sold. Worth noting that if you update the book content at any time or change the cover, you will need a new ISBN, as each number is specific to that one edition published.

If you are an author planning to release on multiple formats and plan to continue writing, then it is best for you to save up and buy a 100 ISBN pack (as a ten pack would run out after a few books).

Remember you need a separate ISBN for each format; you cannot use one number for paperback, hardcover, audiobook etc. It's one for each. I'll mention this again: you do not need an ISBN for audiobooks if you are releasing only on Audible. But if you are on other platforms or publishing it on CD or other physical media, then you will.

Personally, I have my own publishing company for my books, so I wanted that company name registered on all my publication metadata. I bought a 100 pack, which will now probably last my whole career—a worthy investment for my situation.

Book Pricing

This is something where there is no golden rule, only suggestion, and it is your call how you feel your book should be priced for all formats—Please just ensure that you keep your books affordable and in line with other peer books out there. After all, you will sell fewer books priced at $25 when similar books are only $10.

With self-publishing, we need to ensure that bookshops and wholesalers get an incentive to buy our books into their shops and warehouses, and the way to do that is to offer a discount. Amazon, Ingram, etc, all offer discounts on books through their distribution, the standard being 55%. You should not go less than that, as many book buyers will not even look at a book that doesn't offer them at *least* that, as your book needs to make them profit.

Keeping that in mind, this is how I price my books. This is not a guide for you, just an explanation of how you can price yours.

1. Note down the print cost – That is the cost Amazon, Ingram or whoever prices your book at to print. Let us say it's $5
2. Add an additional 55% of that cost onto the subtotal. For this example, it would add $2.75 (as that is 55% of $5).
3. Add profit for yourself. Let us say your wanted cut is $2.
4. This brings the subtotal to $9.75. Round that up to $9.99. Voila!

Marketing Mania

Just because one marketing method worked for one person does not mean it will work for you. Just because placing an Amazon ad sold 100k copies for someone's book doesn't mean that luck will be on your side for your book. No marketing is foolproof or guaranteed; most of it is just a gamble with the odds stacked heavily against you.

It is true that, like all things, the more you are willing to spend, the better your reach will be. You could spend all the money you have getting an advert for your book out there, but there is no guarantee that those seeing it will be converted to buying customers. That is not down to the targeted marketing but the unquantifiable aspect of what catches someone at that moment. The ad may get someone to see your book, but people ignore the majority of online adverts. If this was not the case, then Adblocking apps would not be so widely used, and people would not pay extra to get rid of ads on their computer programs.

Think about it like this, imagine going up to everyone in the street and holding up a book and shouting *wanna buy this?* As you would expect, the take-up would be minimal. And that is more or less what ads are online. The more you pay, the more people who have bought a similar thing will see the ad, but it doesn't mean they will buy them, or that anyone will buy them for that matter. .

You could make it easier and get a company to market your book for you, but unless they are willing to offer you things you cannot do yourself, there is frankly no point. I have seen dozens of companies trying to get indie authors to give them business when all that will be done is a social media blast to an audience of paid followers (I mean, who follows a marketing company to buy new products?) Or they will send a newsletter out to an unspecified audience.

Those I *would* recommend if you wanted to go the marketing company route would be the ones providing author service packages. The ones that offer a wealth of things for a yearly set rate. There are ones out there that, for a small fee, will give you access to marketing courses, Netgalley for your ARCs (see next section for why this is a great idea) and hundreds of dollars worth of social media ads. Basically, if a company lists all they offer, and it is vastly more than you can afford to do yourself, and they are reputable, then they may be worth looking into. Otherwise, you are stuck marketing yourself, but it does not have to be as scary as it seems.

One of the best ways to get your book noticed is something so simple, yet something only some authors consider. Ensure that whatever platform your book is listed on for sale, be it KDP or Ingram or whatever, the keyword tags are as good as they can be. These tags are inputted on all IBNS listings, on Amazon, on all book-selling sites, and anywhere you can buy your book. These keyword tags are critical nowadays, as those are the things that will allow people to stumble across your book online. Just search online for how to find the best keyword tags, and you will find many websites that can show you what to do for free.

Most authors do it wrong by looking at the half a dozen blank keyword boxes in front of them and then just typing in a few simple words that immediately spring to mind. This is a huge, huge error. Let's imagine you are publishing the novel *Dracula*. Most would wrongly use keywords like:

- Love Story
- Vampire
- Gothic
- Suspense

And so on... But they need to look further. They need to develop the keywords into more descriptive phrases. A much more effective way would be something like this:

- Dark romance and obsession
- Vampire seduction
- Gothic horror novel
- Psychological suspense

See how the tags are a bit more developed? Keyword tags are so important, but also something you need to research. For the best tags, you need to consider the whole aspects of your book; the plot, the theme, the character journey, the setting, the tone etc. This is because people search for books with phrases if they are browsing, and the keywords determine if the book will show under that search. The vaguer you are with keywords, the less likely your book will display high up the results list.

Beyond that, getting a social following is a huge addition to any self-published author's marketing arsenal, but that is not for everyone. I have joined and quit most social platforms over the years, as they all gave me anxiety. I was lucky that I found TikTok, as I somehow felt no anxiety with it. (Despite it being videos of me talking). But I have failed at marketing my books on there. I think if all I was doing were that, I would quit too.

Instead of pushing my work, I just started talking. My videos went from 'buy my book' to me giving advice from my experiences of teaching writing, releasing books traditionally, indie to self-publishing. I soon realised that many people needed to hear what I was saying. So I continued, and still do to this day. But I will not pretend I can give you any advice on marketing yourself on social media. I don't know, and I have always been bad at it! Same with newsletters, I have just started my own but have no idea what I am doing. I know authors who swear by them and others who say it did nothing for their sales. At the end of the day, social media and newsletters are only successful if you have exciting content you are happy to put yourself at the forefront of.

If you do not, you will not market well on them.

ARCs

ARCs are no longer what they used to be!

Advanced Readers Copies (also once called Uncorrected Proofs) were books sent out before even the final edit of a book, all for advanced reviews. Nowadays, though, the

ARCs are, by and large, the final edits and the uncorrected proof part is no longer a thing. Even with a big disclaimer on the front page, people will still mark your reviews down if it's not a final draft. I learned this the hard way. I had lots of reviews from one of my books criticising the spelling and grammar when that was already in the process of being fixed. I had a prominent disclaimer on the book stating this, but it made no difference. So with this in mind, it is best not to send out anything until after the final edit.

When you have your digital manuscript ready to go, many new authors need help knowing where to send it. There are a few options for online advance reviews:

Netgalley

The biggest digital review community, but *wow*, they are expensive. A 6-month listing for only one eBook is $499! It is criminal to charge that, but they *are* the biggest community of reviewers, and many major publishers also use them. The community there is great, though sometimes a little jaded.

Book Sirens

Not as big as Netgalley, and they only charge $10 per book and $2 per reader (only readers they find for you, you can invite as many as you want from their community for free). The community there is also great, and the readers are wonderful and full of passion.

Book Sprout

They are cheap at $29 a month for their unlimited package. Though the community of readers is very small, and I have not had much success with them regarding the number of reviews received, , but they are all very nice and friendly.

There are various other digital review companies, but these are the ones I have experience with, so they are the only ones I can tell you about.

Netgalley is the best in terms of community size; there is no question of that. But you can avoid paying $499! as there are cheaper ways to get your books there. BooksGoSocial, for instance, offers access to Netgalley for $99 and gives you lots of social ads and marketing courses. They will put your book on Netgalley under their account, saving you a lot of money. I have had great success with them, and their customer service is excellent. I can definitely recommend them (Though their website is utterly awful.) Of course, other companies offer the same thing, so look into them; just don't get caught paying Netgalley prices when you don't have to.

BUT...

Do not underestimate people like BookSirens. I have got more reviews through them than Netgalley. The reviewers took a bit longer to post the reviews, but they were cheaper overall, so the platform had a better success rate, at least in my case.

Reviews

The best and worst things about being an author.

Getting *any* review for your work is fantastic and quite emotional. Knowing someone not only took the time to read your words but also wrote about it? That is such an honour. But it also is devastating for many authors who are not prepared for any negative comments.

Reviews are just opinions. They are not facts (Unless the reviewer points out actual facts about your book). Their review is what *they* thought. And everyone is different. Everyone enjoys different things. Not everyone will love the same thing as you love. Of course, if a review is slightly negative, it is understandable that you will naturally get carried away and take the words personally. But it would be best if you tried not to do this. At all. It can be a rabbit hole you could fall into and lose all want to carry on the writing journey.

Reviewers don't *want* to hate books. They don't *want* to give less than five stars to anything, but that is not how it is. If you send your book out for review, you must prepare yourself for some bad reviews.

All I can suggest is that you presume that every reviewer will hate your book and give a horrible review. Expect every single review to be one star. As the book is your baby, expecting the worst is the safest place to be. That way, when a good one comes in, it feels that much better.

I have seen authors do lots of strange stuff with reviews. I've seen one author call out a reviewer for leaving them a four-star review instead of a five-star one. I have seen an author try to bully a reviewer into deleting an honest review that was one star. Do not be like these narcissistic brats. Treat your reviewers with kindness, even those who hate what you wrote. Try to look at all reviews in a balanced way. Were they right in what they said? Did they say anything I could address in future writing? Was it just a difference of opinion?

Anti Rule

The *only* time it would be understandable to call out a reviewer would be if their review was racist, homophobic, hurtful, or malicious. But even then, don't be nasty. Don't rise to it. If a review was any of those things, that person is not a reviewer but a troll. They want the blowback. Personally, I would report that review to the platform it appeared in. I would not make it any more public as I would not want to engage with people like that. I suggest you do the same. Try not to give people like that any space in your world.

However, proper reviewers are not like this , and their negative reviews are considerate and polite. A large proportion of reviewers are also authors, so they know how a negative review can hurt but would only give one if they really felt that way. After all, their opinion is their book review brand. They don't hate *you*. They just didn't like your book. Simple.

Never contact your reviewers, either. Only if they contact you first. Any contact can be classed as bullying or abuse. Reviewers do *not* want to contact you. If they did, they would reach out to you first. And there is no point arguing a review. Ever.

If your book has multiple negative reviews, maybe consider their common thread. What in your book is the cause of numerous people being negative? This kind of analysis can help authors in their future writing. I have had some bad reviews that changed the way I approach some scenes in future books in ways I never considered before. Be open to the negativity if there is any.

Above all. And this is for reviewers and authors. Be respectful. Be polite. Be kind. This is not a war. No one is out to get you. A review is an opinion on work, not a slander of the author.

Influencers

This won't take long... If you are on social media and anyone has a video or post that shows you how to *'sell more books with this one trick'* or *'here are the secrets behind publishing to the biggest market'* — Ignore them all. They are liars.

Some have sold hundreds of thousands of books, and they are now telling *you* how you could do the same—excited to find out more? Just save the video, like and subscribe! In reality, these people cannot tell you a thing. They may have sold that many books, but are the books fiction? In the same genre as yours? Aimed at the same demographic? Of course not. 99.99% of the time, these books are how to sell, market or write books. What they do is disingenuous, and they are trying to trick you into following them and buying their book. They are not there to help.

This is why I feel guilty about writing this very book. Even though I am very, very small on

TikTok, I could be seen as some kind of micro-influencer, as people have listened to what I have said about these writing subjects. I know some of those people have even bought this book. (You may be one of my channel's followers!) But this book contains nothing new if they watched all of my videos. Nothing revelatory. It is the main reason this book is short, to the point, and, most importantly, cheap. I am not doing this to fool you. I'm not doing this to steal your money. I am doing this to help those who have not seen my videos and could be helped with the kind of advice I have given.

In summation, don't listen to *any* influencers except me.

Piracy

Finding your eBook leaked onto a torrent site is heartbreaking, but it is not the end of the world. It is relatively easy to get this fixed yourself.

Here is a sample DCMA takedown notice you can use to remove any pirated eBook from a torrent website. There are some important things to note first before sending your email:

- Torrent sites only host links, not the actual file. Getting links removed is easy, whereas removing the actual files is

- impossible, as they are typically hosted on hidden servers.
- All torrent sites have a section about DMCA contact details (either in the menu or in the page's footer). Click on that, and it will tell you where to send your email.
- You cannot send these from free email servers like Gmail, Yahoo, or AOL. A company email is needed. If you have a personal website email, even better! This is because many sites refuse even to read emails if they have been sent from free email hosts. Anyone could be at the end of one of those emails. You can even use a work email address!
- Send your email as plain text with no attachments
- Make sure your email is polite! No swearing etc. No anger. The takedown notice is enough of a threat.
- If they don't reply in a week, send it again. Not replying opens them up to copyright lawsuits, so they usually will act fast, but be aware that they get thousands of these a week.

DMCA Takedown Notice

DATE

Name of website and any contact details listed on their DCMA page

Notice of Copyright Violation (DMCA Takedown Notice), Privacy Violations, and Infringement of Name and Image – Request to Remove Offending Content.

This is a notice in accordance with the Online Copyright Infringement Liability Limitation Act (OCILLA), a part of the Digital Millennium Copyright Act of 1998, requesting the service providers to be held strictly liable for the acts of their users & immediately cease the access to copyrighted material.

I have found infringing material on your website, for which I am the sole copyright owner. I seek the immediate removal of this material from your servers. The detail of this infringing material is as follows:

- **Name of the eBook** released worldwide on **Date of release**.
- **URL where it is officially for sale**
- **Also include URLs to your author page on Goodreads and Amazon etc**

Below is the direct URL for your reference in which you have linked this infringing material:

- **Content Link from their website.**

Under the penalty of perjury, I certify that the information contained in this notification is both true and accurate.

Thank you,

Your name in full

Any contact details

If you need an eBook taken down from any other kind of pirate site that is not a torrent site, you can follow the same guidelines as this.

However, I do not worry about piracy; I prefer to see it as free marketing. Keep in mind that eBook pirates are not your customer base. People who download eBooks from torrents are not people who will spend money. Not to mention that the percentage of people who will download your book is tiny. Of course, it's terrible, but it is a side effect of the digital age, one you cannot avoid.

Your energy is best left to marketing your books to those who *buy eBooks,* ignoring any piracy that may occur. It's not worth your time and worry.

Community

Respect.

This is the key to social discourse in life and as a guide within any community, on or offline.

In online communities, there is enough negativity that you do not need to be a part of. Do not get dragged in by it.

Treat everyone kindly.

Treat them as you want to be treated.

Forgive any rudeness.

Do not engage in hate.

Everyone is equal.

Whether you have published your hundredth or just the first book or even yet to write a word, you should be treated as an equal. You should treat others as such.

When you encounter hurtful negativity, move past it, and please do not dwell on it.

Do not give hate air.

The most common thing that occurs in online forums is abuse. Maybe not intentional, but people regularly post about others, not realising they are talking about real humans—people with feelings.

Even if someone speaks out of line, treat them with compassion.

You may think this is weird to put into this book, but the community aspect is a massive part of self-publishing. Social platforms are the hubs where tribes of fellow thinkers congregate. It is where your book family will be.

Be nice.

Be nice.

Be nice.

Be nice.

Unless it's about Elmore Leonard's writing rules.

Afterword

Thank you for reading. All I can hope for is that at least something in these pages will help you on your writing journey.

This is my parting lesson for you to memorise;

The rules do not always apply. This is *your* journey, *your* story, *your* voice.

Think differently.

Doubt all of the absolutes, no matter where they came from.

Think of the anti-rule instead!

Printed in Great Britain
by Amazon